EYEWIT...
TO 1798

May you be born in interesting times.
ANCIENT CHINESE CURSE.

Edited by
TERENCE FOLLEY

MERCIER PRESS

MERCIER PRESS
PO Box 5, 5 French Church Street, Cork
and
16 Hume Street, Dublin 2

© Terence Folley, 1996

ISBN 1 85635 153 X

10 9 8 7 6 5 4 3 2 1

A CIP record for this book is available from the British Library.

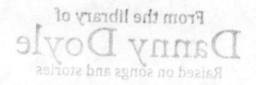

Printed in Ireland by Colour Books Ltd.

CONTENTS

INTRODUCTION

It is necessary to state at the outset that the present volume is not a new history of the rebellion of 1798, nor does it presume to bring new, previously unpublished material to bear on the subject. As its title indicates, it is a collection of various eyewitness accounts of the rising, written by people who experienced the final years of the eighteenth century first-hand. All the narratives in this volume have been published at least once already, but while many of the extracts come from sources probably familiar to readers, the book also contains other passages which will be less familiar, or perhaps unknown to them. These latter have been taken from works that have not been reissued for many years. As we approach the bicentenary year of the rebellion, it seemed appropriate to compile a series of passages from eyewitness sources that would give the reader a general picture of both sides of the conflict, which was not simply a question of Irish versus English. It seemed best to allow those distant Irish men and women to speak to our own time in their own terms, and I have left the passages in their original spelling. It is hoped that this selection of narratives will offer a reasonably clear picture of the nature of the rebellion of 1798. Above all, it is intended to convey as far as the available material will allow, something of the flavour of the period: what it was like to live through those turbulent 'interesting' times. Hopefully, reading the personal accounts of the protagonists of 1798, their humanity will come across before all else. At the same time, the extracts may reveal more clearly to us the issues that once divided them.

For the sake of clarity in the structure of the text, I have attempted to link the passages with short paragraphs dealing with the background to the events and the narratives quoted, making a sort of running commentary to the main body of the book. The linking passages contain my personal ideas on the subject, and they should not be taken as a substitute for wider reading of basic histories or further eyewitness narratives. For convenience, the sources quoted are listed in alphabetical order under authors. The existing bibliography on the period, between historical works of varying tendencies and works of fiction, is extensive, and doubtless the bicentenary will give rise to a considerable amount of additional publications. In the meantime, it is hoped that the present modest contribution will fill a gap and offer general readers sufficient encouragement to undertake further study of the subject.

Finally, I wish to express the following acknowledgements of indebtedness on my part: to my wife, Noel, for her encouragement and constructive comments; to my departmental colleagues, Professor Terry O'Reilly and Stephen Boyd, for their encouragement and interest in the project; to our departmental secretaries, Kay Doyle and Aisling O'Leary, for their patient help and advice in the preparation of the manuscript; to my colleagues, the professional Irish historians, for the instruction and pleasure they have provided over the years.

TERENCE FOLLEY
UCC, 1996

THE GENERAL
BACKGROUND TO 1798

During the seventeenth century, Ireland was the scene of three major conflicts. At the beginning of the period, in 1601, the native Irish and their Spanish allies were defeated at the battle of Kinsale. The English victory meant the collapse of the Gaelic order. In 1603, the defeated chieftains of the north were forced to abandon the country and seek refuge on the Continent, an episode known as 'the Flight of the Earls'. Some forty years later, a civil war broke out in England, between the Royalists and the Puritan faction. Many in Ireland sympathised with the Royalists, who were defeated by the Puritan forces that caused the English king to be executed and who created in England a Commonwealth. The political circumstances favoured an attempt by Ireland to break away from English domination during the period of upheaval in the neighbouring island. For this reason, and also because of the attacks on English settlers by the native Irish, the country suffered the Cromwellian invasion and the ensuing punitive military campaign. A further forty years passed, and once again the Irish sided with the absolute monarchy of James II against the Dutch contestant to the English throne, William of Orange. The Irish suffered yet another defeat, and as a result of the Treaty of Limerick, the majority of Irish landowners were forced to leave the country. Large numbers of them took up employment as soldiers in Continental European armies, and they became known as 'the Wild Geese'.

In contrast with the previous hundred years, the eighteenth century in Ireland experienced no major wars or military campaigns. The remaining native Irish became a dispossessed people almost without leaders. For a time, they were not only defeated, but also demoralised. The English administration based in Dublin was determined to keep them in that condition. All tendencies to rebellion were kept severely in check, especially by means of the anti-Catholic Penal Laws that were introduced from England a few years after the century commenced. In his *A History of Ireland in the Eighteenth Century,* the historian Lecky states that the laws were in the main less harsh than those governing Huguenots in France, or the restrictions imposed on heretics and other dissenters in Spain during the centuries of the Inquisition. Yet he goes on the point out that: 'It was the distinguishing characteristic of the Irish penal code that its victims constituted at least three-fourths of the nation, and it was intended to demoralise as well as to degrade'. In reality, the strictness with which the laws were applied varied from place to place, and the worst aspects of the system were relaxed to some extent by Henry Grattan's parliament in Dublin from about the middle years of the century. Yet in theory if not entirely in practice, the Penal Laws remained in force until well into the following century. Their existence helped to create clear and dangerous distinctions between the Catholic majority and the Protestant minority in the island.

One of the reasons for the official efforts to eradicate Popery from the country, was the continual fear of a revival of the Jacobite spirit that had been defeated in the 1690s. It was feared that the continuing existence of Catholic religious roots among the people, might lead to a revival of the spirit of rebellion against English authority. The original Jacobite ethos was still alive amongst the exiled Irish on the Continent and their descendants, many of them active in the service of armies of nations frequently at war with England. The apprehensions of the authorities appeared to be justified during Bonnie Prince

Charlie's attempt to gain the throne of England in 1745. For a brief but critical moment, even London and the future of the English monarchy seemed to be in peril. Officialdom was also aware that Irish volunteers had fought alongside the Scots during the campaign.

Although the events of 1745 had occurred beyond the shores of Ireland, repercussions of the Jacobite rising were felt also within the island. In addition to the underlying threat of a Jacobite presence, the authorities in Dublin were forced to contend with the existence of secret agrarian societies, especially in the south of the country, from the 1760s (See: Maureen Wall: *Secret Societies in Ireland*, Dublin 1973). Known as the Whiteboys, they were formed principally to protect, as far as their illegal status would allow, the interests of the tenant farmers against the landlords and their agents. On occasion, their activities could lead to local disturbances bordering on open rebellion. The authorities were unable to suppress these secret societies, and by the 1790s further clandestine groups had proliferated, such as the southern Rightboys, and the Peep o' Day Boys and the Defenders among the northern Protestants. At the same time, Grattan's relatively liberal Protestant parliament made various legislative efforts to alleviate the rigours of the Penal Laws. Although such limited measures were doubtless welcome to a hard-pressed tenantry, they fell far short of the ideal of Catholic emancipation. If anything, a limited degree of relief from harsh conditions could help to make the victims of oppression even more conscious of the restrictions under which they were forced to live.

There was a considerable amount of violence at a local level in Ireland during the century, but until the last decade of the period there was no movement which could effectively channel popular feelings into a united cause. While the authorities were engaged in dealing with internal matters, outside the

11

island events took place which exerted considerable influence on historical evolution within Ireland. In the 1770s the North American colonists demonstrated that a determined people could oppose successfully a stronger enemy and throw off irksome foreign rule. Many liberal Irish, with a mind towards national independence, took inspiration from the American Revolution and hoped to emulate the example it offered. During the following decade, the regime of Grattan was moving towards breaking links with England. The creation of the Volunteer militia, ostensibly to help defend the island in the event of an invasion, contributed to the emergence of a set of circumstances that encouraged the proclamation in Dublin of national independence. The public declaration was more an idealistic gesture than a practical step in the political life of the nation. However, it did alert the authorities to a greater degree than previously towards the direction in which national affairs were evolving. It further revealed the increasingly insecure situation in Ireland with regard to England's interests. The American Revolution concerned basically matters of national independence, but in 1789 the revolution that erupted in France brought into play additional factors. The concepts of liberty, equality and fraternity carried with them the radical revolutionary vision of a fundamental reorganisation of the whole of society, including the violent abolition of monarchy and the creation of a secular republic. The new French model became the ideal of an enthusiastic group of Irishmen, most of them young and members of the Protestant ascendancy. In 1791, they founded in Belfast the Society of United Irishmen. For some members, their aim was limited to carrying out the necessary reforms that would offer political and social equality to Catholics. One of the principal founding members, Theobald Wolfe Tone, writes in his autobiography of the question of 'civil rights'. For many other members of the organisation, it proved impossible to ignore the ideological currents reaching Ireland from the Continent. It was not long before the authorities in Ireland began to view the recently created society with hostility, as a hot-bed of subversion and anarchy. A general popular rising in Ireland could be difficult to contain and defeat, but if the Irish were also able to benefit from a direct French intervention, the outcome could easily prove to be a national disaster for England. Even if the Irish struggle for independence were eventually unsuccessful, it would tie England's hands with regard to British intervention in Continental affairs. The French enemy, now led by Napoleon, would be free to propagate their pernicious revolutionary doctrines in other nations. The authorities also feared a rapprochement between the United Irishmen and the agrarian secret societies. The former were active in disseminating their revolutionary doctrine through an oath administered to the civilian populace and even among members of the militia. As they were evidently considered to be the most dangerous of the subversive elements present in the country at the time, the United Irishmen were soon after their foundation declared illegal. The authorities immediately initiated a campaign of persecution and suppression against the known or merely suspected members of the organisation

Military commanders throughout the country were charged with carrying out the policy of search and suppression. The forces at their disposal consisted of the regular army, the native Irish militia, various corps of yeomanry and soldiers in English service. Given a relatively free hand to discover United Irishmen and their supporters, and whatever arms they kept hidden towards rebellion, many of the soldiers and especially the militia acquired a reputation for violence and brutality. Aiding the official forces in their activities were many volunteers from the recently founded Orange Societies.

13

Formed by Loyalist Protestant elements in opposition to the growing influence of the Catholics and, above all, the United Irishmen, these societies soon earned the censure of more tolerant fellow-Protestants, because of their treatment of the Catholic population of the country. A United Irishman who fought in Wexford, Thomas Cloney, recalled how the Orange presence at the battle of Enniscorthy affected the intensity of reprisals after the rebel defeat: '... the rage of the Orange party was unbounded, and ... they had openly threatened the indiscriminate slaughter of all those who were reputed to be disloyal persons ...' Various persons belonging to the ruling classes who were more sensitive to the situation at the time, maintained that the proliferation of Orange Societies, and the behaviour of their members, were causing serious disaffection among the common people. In their willingness to aid and abet the military, the Orange Societies contributed to the creation in Ireland of an atmosphere favourable to insurrection.

Many commentators hold that the military in particular bore a considerable share of responsibility in this respect. The policy of encouraging excesses by allowing a free hand to troops in their search for subversives and arms, had the effect of driving a harassed people deeper into opposition against the authorities. The Catholic Church through its hierarchy condemned the United Irishmen movement, as it had preached against the agrarian secret societies a few decades earlier. This stance had relatively little influence on people who were forced to submit to arbitrary torture, or to opt for rebellion. The introduction of martial law throughout the country in March 1798, instead of further containing the rising tide of rebellion, made matters worse. In his *Personal Narrative of ... 1798,* Thomas Cloney indicates what went wrong with the official policy: 'Martial law defines the duties of the general or inferior officer as clearly as the Statute or Common Law defines the duties of

14

the Civil Magistrate, but, in the year 1798 martial law in Ireland was defined to be the will of the individual general officer, private or drummer, attached to the troops of the line or yeomanry; hence there might be seen at that period in every part of Ireland, where military men were quartered, some victim of private malice or official caprice, writhing beneath the lash of a regimental drummer, or suspended from a gallows, without being previously subjected to the solemn mockery of a Court Martial ...'

PRELUDE TO THE RISING

There were various preliminary stages leading to the actual outbreak of violence in 1798. A particularly important factor in the balance, was the possibility of a military invasion of Ireland by England's arch-enemy, revolutionary France. This would provide sufficient practical aid to the rebel forces, to enable them to take on the Loyalist forces, considerably superior in most respects to the insurgents. When the United Irishmen organisation was proscribed, several important members succeeded in escaping from the country. Given the general ideological orientation of the conspirators, it was natural for many of them to choose France as their place of exile. From there, they continued their revolutionary activities. They attempted to convince the French Directorate of the feasibility of mounting a major invasion force against the English in Ireland. They further claimed that the great majority of the Irish were waiting for a chance to take up arms against the common enemy of both peoples. In 1796, the exiled representatives of the United Irishmen eventually persuaded the French authorities to act on their advice. An invasion fleet was assembled in Brest, carrying troops and arms. In December of that year, it set sail for the Irish coast, reaching Bantry Bay by Christmas. That mountainous region of West Cork was relatively sparsely populated and it was poorly defended against attack. It was hoped to effect a landing and from there to march on the city and port of Cork, linking up on the way with the forces of the United Irishmen. At this point, nature intervened, in the shape of a violent North Atlantic winter gale that continued for days and made a landing impossible. By the New Year, the French fleet was scattered and the ships were forced to return to their home port. On board one of the French warships, the *Indomptable*, Theobald Wolfe Tone recorded in his diaries (later incorporated into his autobiography) his disappointment and frustration at the failure of the French expedition. Because of his well-known involvement with the radical wing of the United Irishmen, Tone had fled Ireland in 1794. He went to America and from there to France, where General Hoche, second only to Napoleon in the military reputation he had earned during the revolution and the ensuing civil wars, became Tone's most convinced supporter. The influence of Hoche was decisive in providing the invasion force and Tone was naturally included in the venture. Although unable to land on Irish soil in 1796, Tone made a further attempt in the wake of the 1798 Rebellion. He was captured on board a French warship, and was imprisoned to await trial for treason. In gaol he committed suicide before the sentence of execution could be carried out. His name has become one of those most closely linked to the history of Irish nationalism, and it is perhaps appropriate that Tone's personal account of the final hours of the abortive French invasion of 1796 should begin the series of extracts that make up this volume:

> The morning is now come, the gale continues, and the fog is so thick that we cannot see a ship's length a-head; so here we lie in the utmost uncertainty and anxiety. In all probability we are now left without admiral or general; if so, Cherin will command the troops, and Bedout the fleet, but, at all events, there is an end of the expedition. Certainly we have been persecuted by a strange fatality from the very night of our departure to this hour. We have lost two commanders-in-chief; of four admirals not one remains; we have lost one ship of the line that we know of, and probably many others of which we know nothing; we have been now six days in Bantry Bay, within five hundred yards of the shore, without being able to effectuate a land-

ing; we have been dispersed four times in four days; and at this moment, of forty-three sail, of which the expedition consisted, we can muster of all sizes but fourteen. There only wants our falling in with the English to complete our destruction; and to judge of the future by the past, there is every probability that that will not be wanting. All our hopes are now reduced to get back in safety to Brest, and I believe we will set sail for that port the instant the weather will permit. I confess, myself, I now look on the expedition as impracticable. The enemy has had seven days to prepare for us, and three, or perhaps four days more before we could arrive at Cork; and we are now too much reduced, in all respects, to make the attempt with any prospect of success – so all is over! It is hard, after having forced my way thus far, to be obliged to turn back; but it is my fate, and I must submit. Notwithstanding all our blunders, it is the dreadful stormy weather and easterly winds, which have been blowing furiously and without intermission, since we made Bantry Bay, that have ruined us. Well, England has not had such an escape since the Spanish Armada; and that expedition, like ours, was defeated by the weather; the elements fight against us, and courage is of no avail. Well, let me think no more about it; it is lost, and let it go!... This infernal wind continues without intermission, and now that all is lost, I am as eager to get back to France as I was to come to Ireland.

I have condensed slightly the above brief extract from Wolfe Tone's autobiography, which represents our principal source of first-hand information about a key episode in the progression towards rebellion. A further eyewitness narrative exists of the expedition to Bantry Bay, which is less well known to English readers – if, indeed, they are familiar with it at all. Over half a century after the ill-fated French voyage, an elderly French statistician, Moreau de Jonnés, published his personal recollections of the incident, as a chapter in his *Adventures in Wars of the Republic and Consulate*. The volume was translated into English from the 1893 edition and published in London in 1920. For anyone aware of the essential facts concerning the French presence in Bantry Bay in 1796, a considerable question-mark must necessarily hang over Moreau de Jonnés' narrative. His text reads like a full-blown adventure story with a certain romantic interest, resembling fiction rather than fact. The author also claimed to have participated in the later French invasion and military campaign in the west of Ireland, in the late summer of 1798. Evidently, by the second half of the nineteenth century, there can have been few contemporaries of the author's alive in France, in a favourable position to dispute his claims. On the other hand, the inclusion of a personal account of the expedition of 1796 in Moreau de Jonnés' memoirs is an indication of the importance which the attempted invasion at Bantry Bay had in France at the time. For that reason alone it is of interest to include here a short narrative of a supposed United Irishmen attack on the military garrison at Cork city, which the author claims took place while the French fleet was tossing in the gale at Bantry, and in which he characteristically claims to have played a leading part:

Our expedition had for its object the city of Cork. No doubt we were not strong enough to attack it seriously, but it had been settled to attack without any precautions, frighten the garrison, and encourage the partizans of the insurgents; and, lastly, to make a military reconnaissance which would clear the way for French troops as soon as they had landed. To this end two false attacks had been prepared, to occupy or divide the attention of the enemy whilst the attempt to carry by direct attack one of the principal outlying posts was made. It was a fortified barrack at the head of a thoroughfare, and defended by a body of infantry who were accused of murdering the prisoners made by them in several encounters. The approaches to this post had been reconnoitred by the English in order to

19

guard against surprise, and advanced sentries made a chain at the foot of the glacis.

In spite of this, our advanced men, skilfully led, availing themselves of the features of the ground, had succeeded in ambushing themselves almost within point-blank range of the sentries, and not more than 200 paces from the barrack. Our leading platoons had got there by creeping, and there they lay on their faces, awaiting the signal to attack. The commander, with his aides-de-camp and me, was led up to the line by a young man who displayed remarkable intelligence and boldness; his name was Sheill. We were posted by him in the interval between two enemy sentries, who must have heard us had not the wind howled continuously. From this advanced post we could see everything. The lights inside the barrack enabled us to make out the entry and even the loopholes on its flanks. These last were a cause of anxiety to me; I had proposed at the council to blow in the gate, which our spies reported to be solid and well defended; but this plan had to be given up for want of the necessary means to put it into execution. Recourse must be had to the simpler but more dangerous plan of breaking in the gate with axes, and volunteers had been chosen from among those offering for this perilous service. The despatch orderlies, who passed from one column to another with wonderful speed, had already informed the commander that all was ready for the attack; and he was in the act of raising his pistol to give its as the signal, when the barrack door opened to allow visiting rounds to come out. The torch carried by the drummer threw a light in front, but it left the officer marching in rear completely in the dark. We could only guess his distance when he replied to the challenge of a sentry. His line of advance led straight for us, and he must discover us and give the alarm if we waited another instant. 'At them, gentlemen!' cried the commander, and at the same instant a shot dropped the officer; for a beam of light reflected from his gorget had disclosed his position and afforded an aim. A furious 'Hurrah!' arose from every thicket, and like the roar of wild beasts could be heard above the storm. On recognising the Irish war-cry, the men of the visiting rounds dashed for the barrack shelter. We were on their heels, and arrived there with them. The door opened to receive them could not be shut, for it was already hampered with bodies. The insurgents, without replying to the gun-fire, flung themselves into the place, and in a few minutes every man of the garrison was slain. The building, on being set alight, was soon completely destroyed by the explosion of munitions stored in it.

However difficult it may be to believe all the incidents narrated by Moreau de Jonnés, his account of the French incursion into Bantry Bay in 1796 could provide the basis for an acceptable film or television script. Partly coinciding with the attempted invasion, another Frenchman, De Latocnaye, visited Ireland and spent several months walking around the country. A refugee from the Revolution of 1789, he bears witness in his travel sketches of the real state of unrest prevailing throughout Ireland in the year before the rising. The following is his narrative of some violent local incidents he witnessed, which formed an integral part of the campaign of containment being carried out by the military against subversives:

I was received with much kindness by Mr Birch, whom I had seen on my first arrival, and I proceeded again to Belfast, where I arrived in time for the celebration of the King's birthday, and heard the volleys fired by the garrison in honour of His Majesty. The people of this town, who were represented some time ago as about to rise, appeared now in a sort of stupor hardly distinguishable from fear. In the evening the town was illuminated, and the soldiers ran through the streets armed with sticks, breaking the windows of those who had not lit up their houses, and of a great number also who had done so. They went into all sorts of holes and corners breaking back windows and the fan-lights of doors. They seized their officers and bore them, in turn, on their shoulders through the streets. The yells, coming from the soldiers, and the huzzas were simply terrible. Three weeks earlier it was the people who assembled tumultuously and made a racket. If I may say it, I think a crowd of soldiers and a crowd of people differ very little in point of the danger to be expected; in the former case, however, if the officers have their soldiers well in hand there is less danger, as by the terror they inspire they are able to prevent the excess to which the populace might give way.

I imagine that the people of Belfast will not long forget the terror in which I found them. General Lake, however, walked the streets the whole night and arrested some soldiers who were becoming unruly; he dispersed the crowd, too, as soon as the time fixed for the illumination was past. The row was so agreeable and entertaining to the soldiers that they would have been very glad to begin it again; a report was, indeed, circulated that there would be a second illumination next day. In every country soldiers are delighted with the chance of making a rumpus, than slashing and cutting they like nothing better, and it required all the activity of General Lake to keep them within bounds.

It is understandable, in the case of an eyewitness who had previously fled from the revolution and terror in his own country, that De Latocnaye's sympathies did not lie with the United Irishmen movement. He maintained that the latter bore a large share of the responsibility for the acts of violence that accompanied the military's campaign of pacification throughout Ireland. The presence of an organisation fomenting rebellion helped to intensify the severity of the repression. Inevitably, the French refugee compared the situation as he saw it in Ireland with recent events in his own country:

Military law was rigorously enforced here on the inhabitants. They were not permitted to have lights in their houses after nine o'clock, and any person found in the streets after that hour was in danger of being arrested. A fair was held during the time I stayed in this little town (Banbridge, Co. Down), and it passed over quite peacefully; the soldiers promenaded through the market-place and obliged women who wore anything green, ribbon or otherwise, to take it off. Had one-fourth of the precaution taken here been observed in France, there would certainly have been no revolution. I was much struck here by the thought of the different results which different characters in government may produce. It is remarkable how in France a weak government and foolish ministers have led a people entirely Royalist to slay a King they loved, and whose good qualities they respected, and to destroy a flourishing monarchy for whose prosperity they had been enthusiastic; while here, surrounded by enemies, a vigorous government in Ireland has been able to repress, and hold in the path of duty, a people discontented and seduced by the success of the French innovations.

The north was the original cradle of the United Irishmen and it is not surprising that De Latocnaye observed both a considerable proliferation of the organisation's influence, and a corresponding degree of harshness in the official attempts to eradicate the growing subversive movement:

The boldness of the United Irishmen increased each day as long as the Government did not interfere; many who had joined them had done so out of fear, and there were with them a number of weak, undecided people ready to range themselves on the winning side, and so immediately on the Government's determination to act vigorously, it was only necessary to let the soldiers appear on the scene, and the difficulties disappeared.

The poor peasant on this occasion, as in so many others, was the dupe of rogues, who put him in the front, and were very careful themselves to stay behind the curtain. The troops went through the country, burning the houses of those who were suspected of having taken the 'Union' oath, or of having arms, and on many occasions they acted with great severity.

Subsequent events were to prove that De Latocnaye's opinion of the courage of the United Irishmen leadership was inaccurate, as was also his evaluation of the efficacy of the policy of repression. He was not in the country during the following year, as matters were reaching a violent head. The United Irishmen conspiracy had spread far beyond the confines of the northern counties. In the extreme south of Ireland, the military were also active in taking preventive measures against potential rebels. General Sir John Moore was charged with the campaign of suppression in West Cork, an area that had proved vulnerable to a possible French invasion only two years earlier. The militia and troops under his command, although frequently posing a major problem with regard to discipline, carried out the task of containing United Irishmen supporters, which, as far as the army was concerned, meant practically the entire civilian population of the country. Moore's personal diaries are a valuable source of eyewitness information of conditions at the time, as seen from an official standpoint. The following incidents took place shortly before the upheaval in distant Wexford, but were apparently recorded some time later:

Bandon, 27th May 1798: I received orders in April to disarm the two Carberries, which is all the country which lies from Crookhaven along the coast to Bandon. Sir Ralph issued a notice commanding the people to deliver their arms to the different magistrates or officers commanding the troops, informing that if they did so they should be not only unmolested, but protected; that if they did not, or persevered in committing outrages, the troops would be sent to live upon them at free quarters, and other severe measures taken to reduce them to obedience. I afterwards issued a similar notice to this for my district, fixing the 2nd May as the date on or before which, if the arms were not delivered in, the troops should act; and to convince them that I was serious, I marched five companies of Light Infantry and a detachment of Dragoons throughout the country to Skull to be ready to act. I expected that upon the appearance of the troops the people would have given in their arms, but it had no effect. I spoke to the priests, and took every pains to represent the folly of holding out and of forcing me to resort to violent measures. I directed Major Nugent, with the troops quartered in Skibbereen, to march on the 2nd May into free quarters in the parish of Coharagh, which had been much disturbed; and I placed the five Light Companies in different divisions from Ballydehob to Ballydevilin, with orders to forage the whole country from Crookhaven to within seven miles of Skibbereen.

My orders were to treat the people with as much harshness as possible, as far as words and manner went, and to supply themselves with whatever provisions were necessary to enable them to live well. My wish was to excite terror, and by that means to obtain our end speedily. I thought this better than to act more mildly, and be obliged to continue for any time the real oppression; and, as I was present everywhere myself, I had no doubt of being able to prevent any great abuses by the troops. The second day the people, after denying that they had any arms, began to deliver them in. After four days we extracted sixty-five muskets. Major Nugent in Coharagh was obliged to burn some houses before he could get a single arm. Then they delivered in a number of pikes. I then removed the troops to another part of the country, always entreating that the arms might be delivered without forcing me to ruin them. Few parishes had the good sense to do so; such as did escaped. The terror was great. The moment a red coat appeared everybody fled. I was thus constantly employed for three weeks, during which I received about 800 pikes and 3,400 stand of arms, the latter very bad. The better sort of people all seemed delighted with the operation except when it touched their own tenants, but whose ruin they saw they themselves must suffer, but they were pleased that the people were humbled, and would be civil. I found only two gentlemen who acted with liberality or manliness; the rest seemed in general to be actuated by the meanest motives. The common people have been so ill-treated by them, and so often deceived, that neither attachment nor confidence any longer exists. They have yielded in this instance to force, are humbled, but irritated to a great degree, and unless the gentlemen change their conduct and manner towards them, or Government steps in with regulations for the protection of the lower from the upper order, the pike will appear again very soon.

General Moore held relatively advanced ideas for his time, as can be seen from the above extract. As a soldier, he carried out his duties thoroughly but without malice, and he was aware that the continuation of the existing social abuses had contributed greatly to the climate of political agitation. Beneath the currents of subversion lay an accumulation over the decades of resentments and grievances, of inequalities and religious conflict. During the period of the Penal Laws, many young Irishmen wishing to be trained and ordained priests had made their way abroad, generally in secret, to attend seminaries in France, Belgium and Spain. In 1795, partly at least as a result of the Revolution of 1789 in France, permission was obtained to open a seminary within Ireland for Irish candidates to the priesthood. Able to study at Maynooth, young Irishmen were no longer in danger of becoming infected with pernicious Republican ideas while abroad. Although still to an extent emerging from a period of repression, the Catholic

Church in Ireland was increasingly encouraged to support the established authorities in the country. This had in general been the fundamental policy of the Church, and earlier in the century the hierarchy and many of the clergy had raised their voices against the agrarian secret societies. In a similar spirit, Church leaders frowned on the emergence of the United Irishmen movement. Being acutely aware of the presence of a strong French influence among the United Irishmen, the clergy were especially apprehensive of the degree to which the movement was spreading among the ordinary people. Their combined verbal condemnation of the conspiracy was as vigorous as the physical attacks against the organisation carried out by the secular authorities. This is attested by extensive documentation, of which the following abbreviated letter from the Rev. Dr Lanigan to the Rev. Dr Troy, Catholic archbishop of Dublin, is a representative example:

Ballyragget, March 10 1798:
Most Rev. Sir – I was absent from Kilkenny these eight days and was a great part of that time occupied with the priests that border on Queen's County, in consulting them, and concerting measures with them, in order to prevent, if possible, the introduction of United Irishmen and their principles into this county ... The priests told me, and I believe them, that fear of assassination prevents them from speaking as much as they wished against United Irishmen. This did not deter me from exposing, at the altar, in the neighbourhood of the Queen's County, their horrid principles; execrating them as well as I could, and warning the poor people not to be deluded by these monsters. I told them that they should rather lose their lives than take the infernal oath of the United Irishmen; and declared, at the same time, that I would prefer death before I would take it myself.

27

Church leaders of the time, having attained a fair degree of toleration for the open practice of the Catholic faith, were acutely suspicious of the United Irishmen ideal of abolishing the distinction between Catholic and Protestant. This was seen, not as granting equal status to both religions, but as the creation of a secular state along the lines established by the revolution in France. The Catholic hierarchy in Ireland were fully aware of the anti-clerical excesses of the Revolution and its violent immediate aftermath. They were naturally opposed to a clandestine society propagating a doctrine that threatened to bring about in Ireland conditions that in once Catholic France, had removed the protection that the Church had enjoyed under the absolute monarchy. The address of Dr Edward Dillon, Bishop of Kilmacduagh and Kilfenora to the Catholic laity of his diocese, and dated 6 April 1798, expresses the anxiety felt by the hierarchy. The general tone of the address is paternalistic, but it sounds a clear note of alarm concerning the nature and extent of the conspiracy. Again, I quote only in part from the original:

> There is not one amongst you, even in the most remote and obscure hamlet, who hath not heard of the oaths and associations which have entailed so many misfortunes on various districts of this kingdom. How many poor exiles from northern counties have you seen arrive amongst you, set adrift, without pity or remorse, by a barbarous association! How many atrocities have you heard committed by persons belonging to societies of, if possible, a still more dangerous tendency! How many villages destroyed, and districts laid waste, in consequence of illegal oaths and conspiracies! It would be foreign to my purpose further to pursue this tale of woe; much less doth it fall within the sphere of my duty to investigate that maze of moral and political causes which have concurred to beget that restlessness and agitation of the public mind which prevails in

28

various parts of the kingdom; suffice it to observe that these oaths and associations have been proscribed by the legislature under the severest penalties. And it would be doing an injury to the opinion which I entertain of your principles to suppose that any of you could be so little acquainted with the obligations which he owes to society, as not to know that you are bound, both by the law of God and the law of nature, to obey the ordinances of the state in all civil and temporal concerns. What could be more deplorable than the situation of that country, in which it would be permitted to each individual to contradict the laws, to withdraw his allegiance, to oppose the legislature! The law of God commands us to obey the rulers of the land. The Saviour of mankind inculcates this doctrine in the Gospel, and the Apostle of nations, the blessed Paul, is clear on the subject.

But, waving these considerations, your own interest, and the happiness of the district in which you reside, call upon you to avoid, with the utmost caution, all illegal oaths and combinations. Take warning from what hath happened in the various parts of the kingdom, which have had the misfortune to experience the direful consequences of those illegal associations. Learn to appreciate the inestimable blessings of peace and tranquillity, which you have hitherto enjoyed. Thrice happy if, whilst the thunder of anarchy growls at a distance, you are allowed quietly to partake of your frugal fare, and compose yourselves to rest without dread of the assassin or the midnight robber.

There are, no doubt, even amongst us, some few whose hearts are corrupted, and whose minds are perverted; who never once beseeched, with humility, the Father of Light to enlighten them; who yet decide every point, philosophize on every subject; whose whole education consists of a few scraps, taken from immoral or impious writers; who, on the authority of some sacrilegious innovator, blaspheme that religion to which they are utter strangers; who, afraid to look into the state of their own hearts, which they have never enriched with the practice

29

of any virtue, and, not daring to look to Heaven, which they have never ceased to insult, would wish to forget themselves in the midst of tumult and confusion. They look forward with anxious expectation for the arrival of their brethern in impiety. They tell us, with a malignant and ill-dissembled satisfaction, that we must not flatter ourselves with the hopes of escaping a visit from the French. I will not take upon myself to determine an event which, as yet, remains amongst the secrets of providence. Obstacles of great magnitude lie in their way. I will not, however, hesitate to declare that the wrath of Heaven could scarcely visit us with a more dreadful scourge. Witness the atrocities which have marked their steps in every country into which they have intruded themselves. Treasures and valuable effects carried off under the name of contributions; the smallest opposition to the will of those apostles of liberty attended with the most horrible devastations; churches pillaged and profaned; our holy religion proscribed; even lately, a respectable nation given up to carnage and slaughter, for having attempted to defend the constitution and laws under which they and their ancestors lived for ages, a brave, frugal, and happy people; the Supreme Pastor of our Church not only reviled and calumniated in the most impudent manner, but also stripped of that property, which enabled him to display a generosity and benevolence worthy of his high station; and to propagate the Gospel of Christ amongst the most remote nations of the globe. Such are a part of the blessings, which, under the specious name of liberty, have been bestowed on many neighbouring countries, by the rulers of the French people ...

In the mean time, let me conjure you, through the precious blood of our Divine Redeemer, whose death we thus commemorate, to have mercy on yourselves, on your children, and on your country; to reject with horror, all clandestine oaths which may be proposed to you. As for my part, it will be the pride of my life, and the greatest consolation which I can enjoy here below, should I be, in any degree, instrumental in preserving you from the machinations of dangerous and designing men. I may surely say, without presumption, that I have a juster claim to your confidence than those workers of iniquity who delight in darkness. The God of all Truth knows that I am a stranger to political parties; and that, in this Address, I am influenced merely by the desire of promoting your happiness, and by the imperious call of a sacred duty.

Events were to demonstrate very soon after the appearance of the above pastoral address, that the weight of Church influence was unable to hold back the rebellion. Whether the people as a whole agreed or not with their pastors, it rapidly became a question of choosing between either submitting to torture or taking up arms and fighting. The possibility of French military intervention in the rebellion remained a nightmare for the secular authorities and the Church hierarchy. As the conflict in Wexford was already nearing its climax, the Rev. Dr Troy, Archbishop of Dublin, issued an address to the clergy of his diocese, dated Whit Sunday 27 May 1798, to be read at all Masses. Dr Troy echoes Bishop Dillon's condemnation of French revolutionary ideology in the United Irish ethos:

> Look at the origin and progress of these detestable doctrines. Their atheistical authors, seeing the intimate connection between religious and civic principles, beheld with the envious malignity of demons the mutual support they afforded to each other for the spiritual and temporal advantage of man; and, accordingly, prepared the dreadful career of anarchy, by the propagation (too successful, alas!) of impiety and licentiousness...
>
> We bitterly lament the fatal consequences of this anti-Christian conspiracy ...

At the time, many of those whose names have since passed into the annals of Irish revolutionary nationalism, by means of song, story and anecdote, were to a large extent still relatively shadowy figures orchestrating a nation-wide conspiracy and preparing the ground for an armed rising. Many of them belonged to the ruling classes of the country and until the actual rebellion enjoyed the benefits of a good social position, in spite of living under the constant threat of arrest and trial for seditious conspiracy. A small army of paid informers and spies kept Dublin Castle more or less up to date regarding the activities of suspected members of the United Irishmen organisation. A leading member of the legal profession at the time, Sir Jonah Barrington, recalled in his *Personal Sketches* how he met a number of conspirators during a social visit to Wexford early in 1798. A committed Loyalist, Sir Jonah held that the Orange Societies were formed by loyal Protestants, with the laudable intention of counteracting 'the turbulent demonstrations of the Catholics, who formed the population of the south of Ireland'. He himself joined one of these societies when, as he puts it, 'I saw that the people were likely to grow too strong for the Crown'. The following extract from his memoirs gives a idea of the progress of the conspiracy at a militant level among the higher ranks of Irish society. A picture also emerges of the atmosphere that accompanies a civil war:

I dined at the house of Lady Colclough, a near relative of Lady Barrington, in the town of Wexford, in April, 1798. The company, so far as I recollect, consisted of about seventeen persons, among whom were several other of Lady B–'s relatives, then members of the grand jury: Mr Cornelius Grogan, of Johnstown, a gentleman of very large fortune, who had represented the county; his two brothers, both wealthy men; Captain Keogh, afterwards rebel governor of Wexford, the husband of Lady B–'s aunt; the unfortunate John Colclough, of Tintern; and the still more unfortunate Mr Colclough; Counsellor John Beauman; Counsellor Bagenal Harvey, afterwards the rebel generalissimo; and Mr William Hatton, and some others. The conversation after dinner turning on the distracted state of the country became rather too free, and I begged some of the party to be more moderate, as our ways of thinking were so different, and my public situation did not permit me, especially at that particular period, to hear such strong language. The loyalists among us did not exceed four or five.

The tone of the conversation was soon lowered, but not before I had made up my mind as to the probable fate of several in company, though I certainly had no idea that, in little more than a month, a sanguinary rebellion would desolate my native land, and violent deaths, within three months, befall a great proportion of that joyous assemblage. I had seen enough, however, to convince me that all was not right, and that, by plunging one step farther, most of my relatives and friends would be in imminent danger. The party, however, broke up; and the next morning Mr Beauman and myself, happening to meet on the bridge, talked over the occurrences of the previous day, uniting in opinion as to the inauspicious aspect of things, and actually proceeding to make out a list of those amongst the dinner party whom we considered likely to fall victims! and so it turned out that every one of our predictions was verified. It was superficial observation alone that led me to think as I did at that moment, but a decided presentiment of what eventually happened soon after took possession of me; and, indeed, so full was I of forebodings, that I have more than once been roused out of my sleep by the horrid ideas floating through my mind!

Bagenal Harvey, already mentioned in this work, who had been my schoolfellow and constant circuit-companion for many years, laughed at Lady Colclough's at my political prudery, assured me I was totally wrong in suspecting him, and insisted on my going to Bargay Castle, his residence, to meet some old Temple friends of ours on the ensuing Monday. My relative Captain Keogh was to be of the party.

I accordingly went there to dinner, but that evening proved to me one of great uneasiness, and made a very disagreeable impression both on my mind and spirits. The company I met included Captain Keogh; the two unfortunate Counsellors Sheers, who were both hung shortly afterwards; Mr Colclough, who was hung on the bridge; Mr Hay, who was also executed; Mr William Hatton, one of the rebel directory of Wexford, who unaccountably escaped; and a gentleman of the bar, whose name I shall not mention, as he still lives.

The entertainment was good and the party cheerful. Temple freaks were talked over, the bottle circulated; but at length Irish politics became the topic, and proceeded to an extent of disclosure which utterly surprised me. With the Messrs Sheers, particularly Henry, I had always been on terms of the greatest intimacy. I had extricated both of them not long before from considerable difficulty, through the kindness of Lord Kilwarden and I had no idea that matters wherein they were concerned had proceeded to the lengths developed on that night. The probability of a speedy revolt was freely discussed, though in the most artful manner, not a word of any of the party committing themselves; but they talked it over as a result which might be expected from the complexion of the times and the irritation excited in consequence of the severities exercised by the Government. The chances of success, in the event of a rising, were openly debated, as were also the circumstances likely to spring from that success, and the examples which the insurgents would in such a case probably make. All this was at the same time talked over, without one word being uttered in favour of a rebellion – a system of caution which I afterwards learned was much practised for the purpose of gradually making proselytes without alarming them. I saw through it clearly, and here my presentiments came strong upon me. I found myself in the midst of absolute though unavowed conspirators. I perceived that the explosion was much nearer than the Government expected, and I was startled at the decided manner in which my host and his friends spoke.

Under the circumstances, my alternative was evidently to quit the house or give a turn to the conversation. I therefore began to laugh at the subject, and ridicule it as quite visionary, observing jestingly to Keogh – 'Now, my dear Keogh, it is quite clear that you and I, in this famous rebellion, shall be on different sides of the question, and, of course, one or the other of us must necessarily be hanged at or before its termination – I upon a lamp-iron in Dublin, or you on the bridge of Wexford. Now, we'll make a bargain! – if we beat you, upon my honour I'll do all I can to save your neck, and if your folks beat us, you'll save me from the honour of the lamp-iron!'

We shook hands on the bargain, which created much merriment, and gave the whole after-talk a cheerful character, and I returned to Wexford at twelve at night, with a most decided impression of the danger of the country, and a complete presentiment that either myself or Captain Keogh would never see the conclusion of that summer.

THE REBELLION IN THE SOUTH-EAST

Following on the uneasy social gathering on that April evening, Sir Jonah made haste to communicate his impressions in writing to the appropriate authorities. He urged on them the necessity of reinforcing immediately the military garrison at Wexford, where he was convinced the rebellion was imminent. It was a vain hope of averting what Barrington considered to be a national catastrophe. At the same time, the passionate exhortations of the Catholic hierarchy failed to influence the course of events. The official policy of suppression, intensified by the proclamation of martial law, worsened an already bad situation. Even the arrest in Dublin in March 1798, of the bulk of the United Irishmen executive, although depriving the movement of an important section of its leadership, did not hold back for long the tide of rebellion. In early May 1798, at various points throughout the country and in a relatively disjointed, ragged manner, the long expected rising erupted against English rule and domination by the Ascendancy. One of those originally active in the United Irishmen movement, William Farrell of Carlow, recorded the events in his native town. The manuscript was edited and published as late as 1949, with the title *Carlow in '98*. The author was taken prisoner, twice sentenced to death and twice reprieved, before the termination of the rising in Wexford. He survived to renege on his association with the United Irishmen. The following extract from his personal memoirs of the rebellion is a description of the rebel attack on Carlow town that failed:

Never before, since the world began, did such an army

march on to take a garrisoned town; a set of trembling, ignorant, country men, headed by an unfortunate, foolish, enthusiastic young man. There was no obstacle in their way to prevent their going into the town; the most trifling one would have done it. Had there been a single sergeant's guard before them, they would never have faced it. Unfortunately for them, there was no such thing and in they marched.

When they came to the potato-market, the place appointed, they halted and commenced shouting, as a signal for all their friends to come to their assistance, but they shouted in vain; the friends they expected were much too terrified with the preparations that were made to stir one inch. When they found this, that they were left alone, they were seized with a sudden panic and some of them proposed to march forward and bring in the Queen's County men but just as they made the movement to go, there were two sentries at the collector's house, a little below them in Tullow Street, and one of them presented his piece and fired and killed one of the party and this single shot stopped the whole body. Then they thought to go through Bridewell Lane and get off that way but just at the moment Colonel Mahon, who had been closely watching them, ordered out a strong party of soldiers from the barrack who, taking them in the rere, had them covered the length of Tullow Street, from the fair green to the potato-market and opened on them a most tremendous fire of musquetry. The scene that followed could hardly be described; they flew like frightened birds; some down Tullow Street towards the Queen's County; some across the potato-market and down Bridewell Lane for the same place and fired at from the windows as they went along. Others were so overcome with fear that they were not able to run away but forced in the doors of about forty thatched cabins that were on the spot, to hide themselves. In vain did Haydon call out to them to stand and fight for their lives; he might as well be whispering to a tempest and was obliged at last to run himself when all was lost and saw his woeful mistake when it was too late. The army advanced, firing volley after volley, till they came up to the cabins that were completely filled with the unfortunate creatures that rushed in. By this time, there was not one of those that came in to be seen in the street, except such as were killed, and they were lying in heaps.

The army, now having no enemy to oppose them, turned their attention at once to the cabins and made short work of them by setting every one of them on fire and all that were in them, men, women and children, innocent and guilty, even all burned together in one common mass. There has been great lamentation made, and very justly, about the unfortunate burning of Scullabogue, but here were forty Scullabogues in Carlow and very little said about it from that day to this. Perhaps those people who justly complain of Scullabogue ought to recollect that it was themselves or their party who first set the example and that there were hundreds of houses burned by them in every direction, and the inhabitants put to death before the deplorable case of Scullabogue happened at all.

In this affair of Carlow, some of the unfortunate people rushed out of the flames, thinking to save themselves, but they were instantly shot or bayoneted and even the people who ran out of their beds with whatever covering they could throw round them shared the same fate. I know one man myself, as peaceable and inoffensive a man as any in town, who ran out of his bed in his shirt and an infant in his arms and was shot dead at his own door for the orders given out were to spare no man that was not in regimentals.

William Farrell entertained no illusions concerning the level of military training among the rebels or the general efficiency of all ranks of the insurrectionaries. To compensate for the lack of training and experience in the civilian population, frequent efforts had been made to obtain recruits to the United Irishmen from the ranks of the militia. These, in the opinion of General

Moore, were mainly a body of men 'formidable to all except the enemy', yet he and other commanders in the field depended to a great extent on such troops to suppress the rebellion. When the actual crisis occurred, the rebel forces found that they could expect little help from the unruly militia, who mostly remained loyal to their commands. If anything, their behaviour towards their fellow-countrymen was more vicious than that displayed by the majority of non-Irish troops during the campaign of pacification. A particular incentive to loyalty, and one quite common amongst all European armies of the time, was the license to acquire booty in the course of military action, from one's fallen enemies or the civilian population of the battle area. The latter frequently bore the brunt of the troops' violent reaction after an engagement, as is attested by the eyewitness accounts of the rising written down by Mary Leadbeater. A member of the Quaker community at Ballitore village, not far from Carlow, she witnessed a military raid on her community shortly after the fight at Carlow town. Troops were sent out to scour the neighbouring countryside for United Irishmen and hidden arms, and as previously elsewhere, they were given a free hand. Their treatment of the civilian population was even worse than on earlier occasions, being intensified by the atmosphere of recent battles:

> This party of soldiers entered Ballitore exhausted by rage and fatigue; they brought cannon. Cannon in Ballitore! The horse and foot had now met. Colonel Campbell was here in person and many other officers. The insurgents had fled on the first alarm – the peaceable inhabitants remained. The trumpet was sounded – and the peaceable inhabitants were delivered up for two hours to the unbridled license of a furious soldiery! How shall I continue the fearful narrative?
>
> My mind never could arrange the transactions which were crowded into those two hours. Every house in the

Burrow was in flames; a row of houses opposite the school was also set on fire; none others were burnt immediately in the village, but a great many windows were broken, and when I heard this crash I thought it was cannon. We saw soldiers bending under loads of plunder. Captain Palmer came in to see me, and was truly solicitous about us, and insisted on giving us a 'protection'. Soldiers came in for milk; some of their countenances were pale with anger, and they grinned at me, calling me names which I had never heard before. They said I had poisoned the milk which I gave them, and desired me to drink some, which I did with much indignation. Others were civil, and one enquired if we had any United Irishmen in the house. I told them we had. In that fearful time the least equivocation, the least deception appeared to me to be fraught with danger. The soldier continued his enquiry – 'Had they plundered us?'

'No, except of eating and drinking.'

'On free quarters,' he replied, smiled, and went away.

A fine-looking man, a soldier, came in, in an extravagant passion; neither his rage nor my terror could prevent me from observing that this man was strikingly handsome; he asked me the same question in the same terms – and I made the same answer. He cursed me with great bitterness, and raising his musket presented it to my breast. I desired him not to shoot me. It seemed as if he had the will, but not the power to do so. He turned from me, dashed pans and jugs off the kitchen table with his musket, and shattered the kitchen window. Terrified almost out of my wits, I ran out of the house, followed by several women almost as much frightened as myself. When I fled, my fears gained strength, and I believed my enemy was pursuing; I thought of throwing myself into the river at the foot of the garden, thinking the bullet would not hurt me in the water. One of the servants ran into the street to call for help. William Richardson and Charles Coote, who kindly sat on their horses outside our windows, came in and turned the ruffian out of the house.

That danger passed, I beheld from the back window of our parlour the dark red flames of Ganin's house and others rising above the green of the trees. At the same time a fat tobacconist from Carlow lolled upon one of our chairs, and talked boastingly of the exploits performed by the military whom he had accompanied; how they had shot several, adding, 'We burned one fellow in a barrel.' I never in my life felt disgust so strongly; it even overpowered the horror due to the deed, which had actually been committed. The stupid cruelty of a man in civil life, which urged him voluntarily and without necessity to leave his home and bear a part in such scenes, was far more revolting than the fiery wrath of a soldier.

As the various local risings were brought under control, the main thrust of the rebellion became concentrated in the county of Wexford. Supporters of the United Irishmen began to crowd into Wexford from the neighbouring counties and more than one peaceful community also suffered from Rebel attacks that echoed the behaviour of the Loyalist troops. In particular, the 'Big House' and its Protestant inhabitants became the objects of the unwelcome violent attention of the hordes passing across the county and away from the pursuing military. For some, it was a question of searching for arms with which to fight against the troops. Others appear to have used the occasion to avenge the burning of their own more humble dwellings by the military. In all cases, the rising was the first opportunity the ordinary Irish people had of openly confronting the all-powerful ruling classes of the country at the time, and they took full advantage of the circumstances of the rebellion to defy authority. The original idealistic aim of the United Irishmen movement had been to abolish for good the harmful distinction between Protestant and Catholic. However, the distinction had been for too long in existence to disappear overnight. The rising, if anything, tended to underline these religious and social differences. The roads leading to the port of Wexford filled with groups of Protestant refugees fleeing before the advancing Rebel hordes, in the hope of finding passage on a ship bound for the safety of Britain. One of those in flight was a member of a Protestant landowning family, Jane Adams, whose narrative of her sufferings and adventures was published by the antiquarian, T. Crofton Croker, as an appendix to his well-known and extensive work, *Researches in the South of Ireland* (London 1824):

All chance of getting a vessel to take us to Wales was over: some of the unfortunate persons who thought themselves happy in making their escape, were brought back to Wexford, and delivered up to the rebels! The large and respectable family of Killeen Castle escaped being put into the common jail only because there was no room for them; but they were put into an old empty house, and a guard placed over them. The first sight that presented itself to them was the Bull-ring (a square in Wexford so called) filled with kitchen tables and carpenters at work making pike handles. Mrs Cliffe has since told me that the captain's wife came up to her on deck, a little after they had got on board, and said, she hoped to be up to her knees in Protestant blood before night! that she had a brace of pistols in the belt of her gown, and swaggered up and down, repeating this horrid wish aloud.

But to return to our own distress. My father bore my intelligence astonishingly, and agreed to return the moment Hayes came for us. The poor fellow lost no time, when the tide answered; and he brought us word that the house was safe, and that no one had returned to it.

We got once more into the boat. When we reached the shore near enough to discern objects, we discovered hundreds of rebels, and, on a closer view, saw that they were all armed. I besought Hayes to turn back to the island; and here I must acknowledge it was my impious hope, that the boat might upset, and end all our cares together. But I had

42

soon reason to adore that providence I had dared for a
moment to distrust. The rebels called out to us to land:
almost petrified with horror, I looked at my poor father
and children, expecting that the moment we landed we
should be put to death. Hayes, with a countenance as full
of horror as my own, endeavoured to quiet my fears: but
what was my surprise, when, the moment I got out of the
boat, a man came up and shook hands with me, desiring
me not to be frightened; that he was Captain Butler, and
would protect me as long as he could; that he would order
a serjeant's guard home with me. 'I know you very well; I
was coachman to Mrs Percival, and you were very kind to
me the last day she went to see you; it was a wet day, and
you ordered me a warm drink'. He then turned round to
select our guard from the hundreds that surrounded him.
They were all contending for rank, wielding their guns,
blunderbusses, and swords, in the most frightful manner.
I expected every moment the contents would be fatal to us,
from accident if not design; they were all drunk. At length
they fixed on the guard to attend us home; one calling
himself captain; another saying he was head lieutenant;
and in mock procession they marched us towards Sum-
merseat; but, before we were half-way, I found myself
unable to proceed, and begged to stop at my neighbour's,
Mr Woodcock's, whose family had first accompanied us to
the island, but had returned, depending on the assurance
of liberty which had been given them. On our arrival at Mr
Woodcock's, we found the family in the greatest conster-
nation and dismay: they had been up all night, at the
mercy of several parties of the rebels, who came repeated-
ly, and examined every part of the house, possessing
themselves of every thing they chose to take. The
moments Mrs Woodcock had to herself she employed in
hiding flour, and anything she could collect in the way of
food, in the chimneys and roof of the house. Many of the
rebels had threatened her, with a pistol at her breast, that
if she had arms or Orangemen concealed, she should pay
for it with her life. Whilst she was tremblingly recounting

this to me, we saw a party, who had joined our guard, approaching towards the house with carts. Mr Woodcock went out immediately to meet them; they obliged him again to open all his barns and offices, (Mr W. was a respectable farmer, and a quaker) out of which they filled their carts with flour, potatoes, etc. Not content with this, they insisted on coming into the house; and crowded up stairs, where Mrs Woodcock and family, with my poor dear father and children, were waiting in terror their departure. On hearing them approach us, I actually pushed my father and children behind a bed, but by the time the rebels reached the room, I dragged them out again, fearing, had they found them hiding, it would have made them more desperate. I stood before them, when again my friend, Captain Butler, came up to me and said no harm should happen to me, and begged I would tell his mistress that, as long as he was Captain, he would protect the house; he believed she had got off to England, but he did not know what was become of his master, the high sheriff; however he was done with that now. The party examined every wardrobe, chest, and closet in the house; and one of them said, on going away, we have used you very well, but the next party is coming to burn all your houses. With what horror did we hear them! We looked at each other, without the power of utterance for many minutes. At length I said any thing was better than to be burned to death, and that we must do the best we could at the island, at least for a short time, till the fury of the day was over. I helped Mrs Woodcock to collect as much as we could take with us; and although our own house was within a few fields distance, I was afraid to venture for any thing belonging to us.

By late May, the main centre of the rebellion was concentrated in Wexford. As the rising gathered momentum, a host of the most varied kind, including members of the Catholic clergy, attached itself to the ranks of insurgents marching along the roads of the county. (Commenting on the presence of priests among the rebels, one of the leading United Irishmen, Myles Byrne, took historians of the period to task for their condemnation of the priests who participated in the rising. He pointed out that none of these historians raised objections against members of the clergy in Catholic Spain who took an active part in their country in the struggle against Napoleon's army of occupation.) Military forces were consequently directed towards Wexford, in an attempt to contain the rebellion. The authorities in Dublin were forced to admit that the task of containment was proving to be unexpectedly difficult. It was disturbing and perhaps galling for Dublin to have to admit its failure so far to suppress a popular rising that was threatening to sever Ireland's connection with England. It required only direct armed intervention by the French, to turn the tide of rebellion in favour of the United Irishmen. Uneasy sentiments of this nature are communicated in Viscount Castlereagh's correspondence at the time, such as, for instance, in the following letter to Sir Thomas Pelham, and dated 8 June 1798:

> The rebellion in Wexford has assumed a more serious shape than was to be apprehended from a peasantry, however well organised. Their numbers are very great, their enthusiasm excited by their priests, and the face of the country so broken and enclosed that regular formations are impracticable. I send you a copy of a letter from Major Vesey, of the county Dublin regiment, an excellent officer, whose account is more detailed than the official despatch from General Johnson. An enemy that only yielded after a struggle of twelve hours is not contemptible. Our militia soldiers have on every occasion manifested the greatest spirit and fidelity, in many instances defective in subordination, but in none have they shown the smallest disposition to fraternise, but, on the contrary, pursue the insurgents with the rancour unfortunately connected with the

nature of the struggle.

Had the rebels carried Ross, the insurrection would have immediately pervaded the counties of Waterford and Kilkenny; as it is, the people are in motion on the Kilkenny side of the river.

General Lake has made dispositions for acting with effect against the rebels in that quarter. Needham is posted at Arklow with sixteen hundred men; Dundas will assemble two thousand four hundred at Carnew; Champagne is at Newtown Barry (Co. Wexford) with nine hundred, exclusive of yeomanry; and Johnson has been reinforced since the action with two regiments, making his strength two thousand.

The enemy are in great force at Vinegar Hill, within half a mile of Enniscorthy, and at Carrickburne, near Taghmon. Their numbers consist of the entire male inhabitants of Wexford, and the greatest proportion of those of Wicklow, Kildare, Carlow, and Kilkenny. From Carlow to Dublin, I am told, scarcely an inhabitant is to be seen.

I am sorry to inform you that our fears are too likely to be realised. I have at this moment an express from General Knox, at Dungannon, announcing an insurrection at Randalstown, where they have taken Captain Jones prisoner, and disarmed the Toome yeomanry. General Nugent had intelligence of this rising, which was fixed for the day on which the Antrim magistrates were to assemble at Antrim to take steps for driving cattle, etc., in case of invasion, and their plan was to seize as hostages. It was intended to send a force to Antrim from Belfast. I hope it may prove a partial mischief, but I much fear the seed has been sown universally, so it will be productive. You know the country so well, and can estimate from the affair at Ross what the intelligence from the north may effect, that it is unnecessary to add any observations of mine.

I understand from Marshall you are rather inclined to hold the insurrection cheap. Rely upon it there never was in any country so formidable an effort on the part of the people. It may not disclose itself in the full extent of its

46

preparation if it is early met with vigour and success; but our force cannot cope in a variety of distant points with an enemy that can elude attack where it is inexpedient to risk a contest.

Viscount Castlereagh and Dublin Castle had ample reason for gloom and pessimism during the critical early days of June, when the future of the English presence in Ireland seemed to hang in the balance. However, the rising in the north was already close to containment and the failure of the rebels to capture the strategic town of New Ross on the river Barrow, was a decisive defeat for them. Viscount Castlereagh was aware of the importance of the Loyalist victory at New Ross. A lively, and at times unusually humorous eyewitness account of the battle for possession of the town comes from a Loyalist noncombatant who in the circumstances and the heat of battle nevertheless found himself drawn willy-nilly into the vicious street fighting. James Alexander apparently took advantage also of the heated sentiments and public interest generated by the rising, to publish his personal experiences of 1798 in Dublin, barely two years after the rebellion. As readers can observe from the following narrative of the battle of New Ross taken from his book, the author's exuberance pervades his text, in spite of the carnage he describes:

The battle commenced about five o'clock. I did not awake until half past six, when I was rouzed by the reports of detached vollies, and some very heavy running fires of musqettry, drowned at some periods by the roaring of cannon; and every little period of cessation filled with huzzas. Expecting a dismal scene of terror and confusion below stairs, I did not rise till nearly about eight. In about half an hour or less, afterwards, I went down stairs and opened the door, expecting to see some soldier who would procure me a red coat, arms and ammunition. The Ross and

Mid-Lothian cavalries were drawn up just before me. Captain Tottenham of the Ross cavalry asked me 'what news?' I told him I was just out of bed, but that I perceived, my last night's news was in loud circulation. He smiled and requested I would go and take a peep into the Main-street and see what news? I believe the captain was only jesting: for he could hardly think I should prove such a madman. However upon some of his men observing that they understood I was an old soldier, and had been in several engagements last war – fired with the charming compliment, off I ran to the Main-street directly; though followed by peals of laughter!

Completely to remove the smallest appearance of boasting, I must here ingeniously declare, that I had no idea of any part of the battle being within the town walls, (as the ruins are still called) otherwise I should not have acted so madly. And I never once bethought myself, on this occasion, of the necessity of a military uniform and accoutrements, to preserve me from the king's troops, who were much less likely to spare a man in my garb than the rebels themselves.

As I approached near the Main-guard, which was stationed at the Court-house in this street, some of the remoter soldiers called to the rest, 'Shoot that fellow! Stick him!'

I laughingly exclaimed, 'ye bloody-backs!'

Upon this two men levelled at, and no doubt would have shot me, but for the interference of some of my last evening's guard, who mentioned the general's friendship for me, as though it were particular. I passed by and was going further up the street, when my good friends called me back; but the rest bid me 'go on and fear nothing', expecting as I was afterwards told, that I should be shot! Still I advanced up the street, but not halfway when I heard a close bustle of I knew not what, as the street was so incurvated that I could not see. All this time a remote firing went on, but not without some intermission, which space was filled with huzza. I advanced now but slowly, straining myself to see as far up the street as possible, without the hazards of advancing too far. Presently I heard a hasty muttering of about twenty voices and a rattling which I naturally and justly conjectured to be cannon wheels. Five or six muskets more went off. They were succeeded by two, then by about four; then about a dozen; and at last a heavy shower for about one minute. This was at the church-lane. At last a piece of ordinance went off, which was followed by a fearful shout of one party and a triumphant huzza of another. I was still on the gape, and making long strides. A very loose firing of musquetry now began again, and a party of rebels appeared stalking down the street, in attitudes not unlike my own. I turned about in order to alarm the guard; but lo! a strong body of the king's troops with Grumbling Bess, a roaring nine-pounder, stopt up the lower part of the street, not quite as high as the shambles, and the rebels made a stand just above the belly of the curve; so that one party could hardly see the other. In this extremity what could I do? I got close up against a shop door exactly facing Bake-house-lane. This was the house of Mr Dowsley, an eminent Loyalist of whom I shall have occasion to speak by and by. On each side of me were bow windows, by which I was completely concealed from both parties. Now a dreadful pause took place, neither rebels nor soldiers fully appearing to each other. I popt out my head, and asked the rebels if I might pass through them? But an old, strong, well-made man, in a very wretched trim lift up his clumsy withered claw and shook it at me exclaiming, Fon! Fon! Fon! I took his advice and kept close. Mean time the soldiers advanced in front of their cannon. The rebels also began to shew themselves. A few musket shots were exchanged on both sides. Two rebels dropt, and one was wounded; and began to howl like a Chicksaw Indian when he hears the war-hoop *(sic)*. But very few of the shots on either side were fired with proper judgement. Most of them owing to the cowardly positions of some, struck against the walls of the hollow side of the street. I now observed an important circumstance, which I hoped to tell

49

the main-guard: the rebel balls flew (comparatively speaking) amazingly feeble. Hence it was evident that their powder was wretchedly inferior to that of our troops. I have been since told that it was manufactured for them at Wexford. But alas! this was a miserable time for making observations; and it was hardly probable that I should ever escape alive to communicate them to my loyal friends. Still a shy firing was kept on, without any further effect; but at last both parties as if by mutual consent, appeared full in each other's view. Never was I more fired with the ardour of battle than now. What would I not give, to make one amongst the soldiers, even though I were sure to fall! Both parties began a clumsy sort of fire, when, suddenly the soldiers opening their cannon upon them, blew numbers of them off their legs; amongst whom was my friend Mr 'Fon, Fon!

The above passage is an unusual picture of a street battle from the very centre of the combat, as witnessed by one who was evidently regarded by his own side as something of a comic nuisance. Alexander also very nearly paid with his life for his sanguine curiosity, when a soldier mistook him for a Croppy on seeing him in the street in the 'coloured', or dark clothes that contemporaries often refer to in their narratives. After a series of close shaves, the author made his way back to captain Tottenham, with '... more news than I have time to relate, or you to hear', as he ruefully informed the latter. Apparently having learned from his recent experiences, Alexander opted to remain indoors until the battle had passed beyond the town. The battle had waged for several hours, and eventually the action had become sufficiently distant to permit the author to indulge his curiosity viewing the aftermath of the slaughter:

Exactly at half an hour after two, some of my brave and humane friends in tribulation called on me, and told me, that the battle was now too remote to affect the town; that, for their parts, they were too much fatigued in the late des-

50

perate charge, to follow on; but that, if I chose I might now come under their protection and see the town and the slain. I did so, and saw the streets literally strewed with dead carcasses. The greatest slaughter was in the Main-street, especially near the Church-yard. The piece of cannon planted on an eminence just above the Church-lane, did very much the greatest execution of any other. Next to the Main-street, the greatest slaughter was around the Town-wall, where the battle raged. Next, the Chapel-lane, 'twas horrible; next, Brogue-maker's-lane, Michael-street and the Cross-lane; in all of which lanes the number of slain on the same length of ground was pretty equal; with this exception that, in the Brogue-maker's-lane, many were burned to ashes, of which we could have no knowledge or conjecture, but from many carcasses reduced to a cinder, some of which were partly reduced to ashes. Amongst the slain in the Main-street, I saw bodies with frightful wounds of about one fortnight's standing, evidently distinguishable from those received on this day. It is almost incredible that men with such large deep raw wounds, could bear the fatigue even of their march from Wexford or Enniscorthy. Some of those gashes were nearly, if not entirely, to the bone, and six inches long! I speak moderately. What infatuated desperadoes! Scarcely any of them, but piously wore Scapulars. Mr Wheatly, of the Ross infantry, took off hundreds of them, and shewed them with as much glee as an Israelite in King David's time might be supposed to exhibit as many foreskins of Philistines! One of the Insurgents, not having sufficient faith in his Scapular, hung a pewter dish about his neck with a string! But neither his shield nor his Scapular could save him. The dish was bored through with a musket ball, and his body too!

One piece of superstition I saw, which I believe is not easily equalled, even by Borlasque. On the belly of a half-roasted rebel (of which there were very many-roasted to death in their own fires) at the entrance of Chapel-lane, lay a Roman Catholic prayer-book open at 'The office for the dead'. This, I suppose, was piously designed that the Divine being himself should read the prayers 'for the soul of the faithful departed' I will tell you why I think so. I took the book in my hand, and opening it at 'an act of charity' restored it to its former place; on which an innocent, but heavily afflicted young woman (at least in appearance) modestly and respectfully reproved me. Then carefully turning over the leaves till she found the former place, she pressed the book open, and laid it on the heart of the corpse, as at first. I laughed a little, at which one of the soldiers looked much displeased, and left me!

The extracts from James Alexander's narrative have been quoted to some length, as they communicate in a revealing way the flavour, so to speak, of the moment. His account also reveals, deliberately and unconsciously, some essential aspects of the mentality of the period, in addition to providing a close-up view of one of the principal military encounters of the campaign in the south-east of the country. It is of further interest to compare Alexander's account of the battle of New Ross, with a similar picture from the rebel camp, of the battle of Ballyellis. This took place some time later in the rising, shortly after the decisive final encounter at Vinegar Hill. Although the latter was a telling defeat for the United Irishmen, the combat at Ballyellis showed that the Rebel forces were still capable of reserving a few unpleasant surprises for the exultant Loyalists. The following account, more serious in tone than that of Alexander, comes from the personal memoirs of the rebellion by one of its leading commanders in the field, Joseph Holt, who led the Rebel forces at the battle. It should also be mentioned that later commentators have cast considerable doubts on the protests of innocence expressed by Holt, who claimed that the personal spite and persecution of his enemies drove him for refuge into the ranks of the United Irishmen. For one who portrayed himself as a victim of circumstances, Holt displayed notable talents as a commander in the field, and a clear willingness to put his talents at the disposal of the rebellion. Many United Irishmen leaders like Holt were executed when the campaign ended, but he himself was one of those deported to the recently established penal colonies in Australia. It is also necessary to point out that some doubt has been cast on the accuracy of Holt's own estimate of the casualties of the battle of Ballyellis, especially those he claims for the Loyalist cavalry:

I ordered all the officers to be at the head of their respective corps, to form them twelve deep, and then to wait for orders. The enemy were about a mile distant at this time. I then ordered five hundred of the best musket men to form my advanced guard, and one thousand pikemen to follow close. I next examined the road by which the enemy were to advance, and soon determined on the point where we would receive the enemy. I caused three horses in cars to be placed across the road, and fastened them securely, so as to obstruct the passage, and stationed one hundred musketmen behind them. I had one thousand musketmen in reserve. The hedges on each side of the road were thick and strong of crab and thorns, and the dykes five feet deep, so that a man could scarcely appear above them. I ordered the pikemen to make passages in the hedges, so that they might easily retire, or advance as occasion should require: and soon had all my preparations complete. With my advanced guard I met the enemy, keeping all my other people out of sight, and commenced firing, and then we retreated as fast as we could, as I had directed, and every thing had the appearance of a panic.

The enemy who were cavalry, were sure they had it all their own way, but had to push on and cut all down before them, and they advanced upon us bravely, but with too much confidence. When they reached the cars, I brought my musketmen round upon them, who fired on their rear with murderous effect, put them into disorder, and they

53

finding themselves surrounded and falling in great numbers, were in a real panic. The pikemen now advanced through the hedges, and on my reserve coming up behind them, it was all up with the King's troops, and in less than twenty minutes, there were three hundred and seventy of them slain. Our loss was but four wounded. A black trumpeter was most tenacious of life, he took more piking than five white men. Before he expired, a fellow cut off his ears for the sake of the gold rings, and put them in his pocket. The trumpeter, during his torture, exclaimed ... passwords of a United Irishman.

I saw a young boy from one of the dykes pass his pike into the side of a soldier, and could not extract it again; the soldier fell dead. The boy took from his pocket a purse with thirty-five guineas in it, some of the plunder he had made the day before. One of the boy's comrades instantly seized the purse, and tried to take the money from him. He cried out to me, and I caused his well earned prize to be restored; he presented me with it. I kept it for him, till I gave it to his father, one Gough, who lived near Clone, the residence of Charles Coates, Esq.

In this action, a horse of one of the soldiers received a wound of a pike in the haunch, which made him carry himself and rider over the barricade of cars we had formed in the road, and thus he escaped to Carnew Malthouse, in which there was a company of infantry, who kept up an incessant fire upon us. I examined the place, and found it impossible for us to get at them to expel them. I, therefore, determined to make a feint of retreating towards Slievebuoy, hoping they would leave their fortress, which they accordingly did, and made a pretence of following us, but as soon as we gave them a volley, back they fled, and it was 'The devil take the hindmost'.

There is a certain element of poignancy in the image of Joseph Holt recalling in distant exile as a felon, his moments of glory in the rising. He comes across in general as an able commander of troops, who led rebel forces in Wexford and afterwards led them in retreat to the Wicklow mountains, accompanying other commanders, such as Myles Byrne. There was undoubtedly an element of satisfaction in the fact that his troops inflicted a defeat on the Ancient Britons, a body of cavalry that had become notorious for their brutality. Holt's passage further illustrates the extent to which experience had enable the untried mob from the first days of the rising, to develop into a fighting force that could hold its own against a trained, well armed enemy. He made good use of the rebels carrying the long pike that subsequently became the traditional Croppy Boy symbol of 1798 – despite the fact that for the rebels of the time, the pike was considered to be a weapon lacking the status that was conferred on one by the possession of a firearm.

Many European armies of the period, including the English army, had corps of pike soldiers, who could perform effectively in certain conditions. Such favourable circumstances for the Rebel force were not present at the decisive final encounter at Vinegar Hill, outside the town of Enniscorthy. Here the insurgents were hampered by their vulnerability to cannon fire and by the poor state of preparation in their defences. A first-hand account of the battle comes from the personal memoirs of the rebellion of one of the principal United Irishmen leaders, the Wicklowman, Myles Byrne. He not only took a leading part in the Wicklow campaign and in the retreat back to his native mountains, where he helped to hold off the enemy for a period of time, but he also managed to escape to Dublin. There he became involved in Robert Emmet's renewed United Irishmen conspiracy, leading to the abortive rising in the city itself in 1803. After the defeat of Emmet's short-lived attempt to revive the spirit of '98, Byrne succeeded in escaping to exile in France. His recollections of the agitated period, under the title of *Some Notes of an Irish Exile of 1798*, include the

55

following narrative of the last major stand by the rebel forces in Wexford at the battle of Vinegar Hill:

At break of day the different corps began to quit their bivouacs, each to repair to the position assigned to them on the hill and on all the roads leading into the town of Enniscorthy. Our wounded men, that we had transported with us from the county of Wicklow, in order to have them placed in the hospital, we left at Drumgold, one of the suburbs of the town under Vinegar Hill; we had also to leave there a vast number of women and young girls, who had followed their husbands and brothers, to escape from the English monsters who were devastating their homes. All this caused a sad embarrassment, no doubt, to our column, but by no means damped the courage of our men; on the contrary, if anything was required to rouse them to deeds of valour, it was this occasion to protect these innocent females, their dearest ties to life. What a heartbreaking scene to witness the separation which here took place at the dawn of day, husbands quitting their wives, brothers their sisters, never more to meet.

Skirmishing at our advanced posts commenced with the day; however the battle did not become general on the whole line before seven o'clock, but at day-break several shots were heard in different directions from the enemy's camps. These were signal guns, which proved to us that we were now nearly surrounded on all sides, except the Wexford one which should have been occupied by General Needham, it was said, had he followed his instructions. This is mere twaddle; he remained in the rear, in reserve, by the orders of his General-in-Chief, Lake, to keep the road open to Gorey. This prudent English general, who refused to fight us at Kilcavin Hill, did not like to risk a charge of our pike-men, without having a division in reserve to fall back on, in case of defeat. His powerful artillery commenced a tremendous fire, which was for some time directed against the summit of the hill, which was considered our strong position, where it was thought our men were massed, ready to be brought into action. Our small artillery, in answering the enemy's great guns, soon expended the last round of ammunition, and to very little effect. We wanted Esmond Kyan here to command it, as he did at the battle of Arklow, but unfortunately this brave officer had to remain in Wexford to get his wound cured. To remedy instantly the bad effect which the ceasing of our artillery might produce, a large column of chosen pikemen was formed, composed of the county of Wicklow men, Monaseed, Ballyellis, Gorey, corps, etc., to attack the enemy's left flank, and, if possible, to turn it and to bring our pikemen into the action; which now appeared the only resource we could count on, for our gun-men had also nearly expended their scanty supply of ammunition. As to defending the intrenchments that were raised on the hill, it would have been quite ridiculous to have attempted it, they not being more than a couple of feet high in many parts.

I had not seen Vinegar Hill since the morning after the battle of Newtownbarry, the 2nd. of June, and I was surprised to find that scarcely anything had been done to make it formidable against the enemy; the vast fences and ditches which surrounded it on three sides, and which should have been levelled to the ground, for at least a cannon-shot, or half a mile's distance, were all left untouched. The English forces, availing themselves of these defences, advanced from field to field, bringing with them their cannon, which they placed to great advantage behind and under the cover of the hedges and fences, whilst our men were exposed to a terrible fire from their artillery and small arms, without being able to drive them back from their strongholds in those fields.

Several columns of our pikemen, however, were instantly brought to attack the enemy's formidable position behind the fences in the fields, and it was in leading on one of those desperate charges, that the splendid Dan Kervin was killed, at the head of the brave county of Wicklow men. His death at this moment was a severe loss, though he was soon replaced by a leader equally brave; yet his men could not be easily roused from the gloom cast over them by this misfortune; besides many fine fellows, their comrades, fell at the same moment beside Kervin. Indeed, it is a miracle how the other chiefs escaped; they all displayed the greatest coolness and courage, charging at the head of their men under the tremendous fire of the enemy's batteries, which were sending cannon-ball, grape-shot, musket-ball, as thickly as a shower of hail-stones.

I had been in many combats and battles, but I never before witnessed such a display of bravery and intrepidity as was shown all along our line, for nearly two hours, until our ammunition was expended. It was then recommended by some of our chiefs to assemble all our forces and attack the enemy's left flank, overturn it and march back to the county of Wicklow.

More than a few of the United Irishmen leaders were aware that the defeat at Vinegar Hill spelled the end of the rising in the south-east of the country. The Dublin based English authorities were equally aware of the turn that their fortunes had taken in the Wexford campaign. The official correspondence of Viscount Castlereagh at the time exudes a considerably more positive note than some weeks previously, although the sense of jubilation is also tempered by the confession that commanders in the field were experiencing considerable difficulties in containing the violence of their own troops and those helping to root out the rebellion. For many who had lived for weeks in terror of the insurgents, their fears had been replaced by a desire for vengeance and reprisals became an integral part of the army's mopping-up operations in the area:

From Lieutenant-General Lake to Lord Castlereagh: Enniscorthy, June 21 1798: My Lord – I am rejoiced to send you the enclosed account, which I hope will please your

Lordship and the country in general. The troops behaved excessively well in action, but their determination to destroy every one they think a rebel is beyond description, and wants much correction. You will see, by the enclosed letter and address from Wexford, what an unpleasant situation I am led into by Lord Kingsborough. My intention is at present to march near Wexford tomorrow, and insist upon their leader being given up, which I think myself obliged to do, according to orders issued by Government, and more particularly so, as the people of Wexford have done much mischief. It seems somewhat extraordinary that the address should have been signed by Mr Keogh.

I address this to you, thinking Lord Camden might be gone. If he is not, I will beg my best respects to him, and that you will believe me, with great truth, etc. G. Lake. I write in great haste.

Castlereagh replied with equal haste to acknowledge receipt of the good news for English authority in Ireland:

Dublin Castle, June 22 1798: Sir – I have had the honour of receiving your despatch dated Enniscorthy, the 21st. June, with I have laid before the Lord Lieutenant. His Excellency will express to you his approbation and satisfaction at everything you have done, and I sincerely congratulate you upon your success at Vinegar Hill.

I consider the rebels as now in your power, and I feel assured that your treatment of them will be such as to make them sensible of their crimes, as well as of the authority of Government. It would be unwise, and contrary, I know, to your own feelings, to drive the wretched people, who are mere instruments in the hands of the more wicked, to despair. The leaders are just objects of punishment; and the situation of the rebel army such, that you may fairly make the terms you give them rather an act of voluntary clemency than conditions extorted by the rebels with any prospect on their part of successful resistance. I need not add more. The Lord-Lieutenant will himself convey to you his sentiments.

Military post, even in those days of relatively difficult overland travel, was obviously a matter of exceptional haste and priority. On the same date as the above letter from Dublin, General Lake was acknowledging correspondence received from Castlereagh:

> Wexford, June 22 1798: My Lord – I received yours, and return you many thanks for the information of the two regiments of militia from England. I sincerely hope they may soon return, as this country will soon be settled; as I believe the lower order of people are heartily sick of the business, and are abusing their leaders most completely, and will bring in their arms in a day or two; in short, I have every reason to hope that a few days will settle the business here.
>
> I have taken Hay, one of their commanders, yesterday. He will be tried this evening, and most probably executed. If I hear of any assembly of men, you may depend upon their having a complete drubbing; but I strongly suspect they will not try the chance of another. The carnage yesterday was dreadful. The rascals made a tolerable good fight of it. In great haste, most faithfully yours, G. Lake.

The general wrote again on the following day to Lord Castlereagh:

> Wexford, June 23 1798: My Lord – I have every reason to think matters will be settled shortly to the satisfaction of Government. I believe we shall have most of their generals. Roach has been tried this day, and will be executed, as will Keugh, who was both general, adviser, governor of the town, etc. I really feel most severely the being obliged to order so many men out of the world; but I am con-

vinced, if severe and many examples are not made, the Rebellion cannot be put a stop to. I believe Cooke knows a great deal of Keugh. I am in great hopes of catching Bagnell Harvey. A Mr Grogan, a man of £6,000 per annum, is just brought in; what there is against him I don't exactly know; I imagine sufficient to convict him. It has been suggested to me that the surest mode to prevent people in such circumstances concerning themselves in these acts of violence would be to forfeit their estates; but, as I have no wish to visit the sins of the fathers upon the children, I shall not think of proposing such an act, but wait your orders upon the subject.

I will beg you to forward the enclosed to Lord Camden, whose departure I most sincerely regret for every reason, and particularly so as he would have enjoyed seeing an end to the Rebellion – a time which, in my opinion, is not far off.

I hope all things are going on well about Dublin. I suppose Sir James Stewart has given in his resignation; he seems very angry with me. Yours faithfully, G. Lake.

The victorious troops in general and, especially, the yeomanry and other Loyalists who volunteered at this late stage in the rebellion to aid in the suppression of the remaining pockets of insurgents, certainly did not share in any way their commanding officers' reluctance to pursue viciously their defeated enemy. General Lake was, characteristically for a man who respected property, unwilling to contemplate wholesale confiscations, such as had been the norm during the seventeenth century. His fair-minded sentiments were echoed by General John Moore, hurried from Cork with his forces in order to help put down the rebellion, and still conscious of the degree of responsibility which the ruling classes bore for the entire affair. The Loyalist rank and file had little sympathy for Viscount Castlereagh's compassion for the 'wretched people' duped into rebellion by their United Irishmen leaders. Most of the accounts of atrocities inflicted on the civilian population in the wake of the rebellion, passed into popular oral history. Published narratives came mainly from the Loyalist side in the struggle, and these contained, as one would expect, little reference to the great number of excesses committed by Government supporters. Over two decades after 1798, a Brother Luke Cullen attempted to compile a series of unwritten narratives of the aftermath of the rebellion in the south-east, from surviving eyewitnesses in Wicklow. His manuscript was published over a century later by *The People* Newspapers, Ltd., Wexford, from which the following account is taken of a incident in which a company of the Ancient Britons, apparently still smarting after their defeat at Ballyellis, enticed a group of farm labourers towards the road, where they shot many of them dead and then took off in full pursuit of the survivors, as if taking part in a fox-hunt:

> The carnage was now for a short time changed into a perfect and uproarious hunt. They were not much at fault during the chase, and the fleetness of their steeds, their tenacity in the saddle, and skill in directing the movement of their charges, enabled them soon to come up with the fugitives, each one of whom they despatched, although they had a long chase after some of them.

Atrocities had not been limited to one side alone during the rising. On the rebel side, there were two notorious incidents which incited Loyalists' desire for revenge and chastisement of their enemies. One especially gruesome episode was the burning of a barn at Scullabogue after the defeat at New Ross. All the Protestants imprisoned in the building perished, but some account of the incident comes from the rebel side, in the personal recollections of Thomas Cloney:

The wretches who burned Scullabogue barn did not at least profane the sacred name of justice by alleging that they were offering her a propitiatory sacrifice. The highly criminal and atrocious immolation of the victims at Scullabogue was, by no means, premeditated by the guard left in charge of the prisoners; it was excited and promoted by the cowardly ruffians who ran away from Ross battle and conveyed the intelligence (which was too true) that several wounded men had been burned in a house in Ross by the military.

The principal difficulty in recording atrocities of this nature, is the absence of eyewitness narratives. If there are no survivors, as is unfortunately often the case, the perpetrators of such crimes are silent on the matter. Whereas the incident at Scullabogue lacks direct eyewitness evidence, the other major rebel-instigated atrocity of the rising has been narrated in some detail by one of the potential victims, who evaded execution at the last moment, by the arrival near Wexford of General Moore's troops who took the town the next day. Charles Jackson was a Protestant glazier known for his Loyalist sympathies, who failed to escape by sea from Wexford and was imprisoned to await execution. He possessed no heroic qualities and at one moment he was forced to carry out himself the execution of a fellow-prisoner. This was shortly before he and a number of others were brought out and taken to Wexford bridge, where public executions had previously taken place and where the rebel horde attempted to emulate the excesses of the terror in revolutionary France:

Two days passed without my being particularly noticed; but, during that period, many prisoners were taken out, a few at a time; and, being carried to the camp, were piked. On the day that information was received of the rebels being defeated at Ross, to revenge the loss, fifteen of the

Wexford, and ten of the Enniscorthy people, were ordered out of the gaol. When this notice was given, I ran into my cell, got upon my knees in a dark corner, and pulled some straw over me; but a man of the name of Prendergast, came in and drew me out, uttering shocking threats against me. He dragged me into the yard, where I found my unhappy comrades upon their knees. One of them, who had been a Protestant, but had become a Catholic, and who was now imprisoned on a charge of being an Orangeman, requested to have the priest with him before he died. This was immediately granted and a messenger was sent to Father Curran, the Roman-Catholic parish-priest of Wexford. He presently came; and, to give effect to his admonition and intercession, had dressed himself in his cowl, and bore a crucifix in his hand. He held up the crucifix, and all present fell on their knees. He exhorted them in the most earnest manner; he conjured them, as they hoped for mercy, to shew it: he made every possible exertion to save the lives of all the prisoners: but it was in vain. He said, he could witness that the Wexford people had never fired upon them or done them any injury, but that he could not again say mass to them if they persisted in their cruel resolutions. At last, he influenced them so far as to prevail upon them to return to the gaol the fifteen Wexford men; but for those from Enniscorthy, he could obtain no remission.

With hearts overflowing with gratitude to the Almighty, we went back to our confinement, and in that state remained, every day seeing more prisoners brought in, and others taken out to be massacred, each of us apprehending it would next be his lot. On Wednesday, June 20, about eight o'clock in the morning, we heard the drums beat to arms and the town-bell ring, which was a sure sign of our friends being near; but, at the same time, we expected we should be cut off before they could arrive and release us. In this terrible state of suspense we remained until four o'clock in the afternoon, when we heard a horrid noise at the gate, and a demand of the prisoners. Eighteen or twenty were immediately taken out; and, in about half an hour, the rebels returned for more victims. In the whole, they took out ninety-eight. Those who were last called out were seventeen in number. Mr Daniels and Mr Robinson, both gaugers; Mr Atkins, a tide-waiter; Mathews and Gurley, who were with me at the execution of Murphy; and myself, were included in this lot. The moment Mathews put his head out of the gaol, he was shot dead; which, I believe, would have been the fate of us all, had not a Mrs Dixon (wife of a man who kept a public-house in the town, and who had been made a captain by the rebels) when Mathews fell, immediately advanced, and desired they would desist, as they ought to allow the people on the bridge the pleasure of seeing us. We were accordingly marched to the bridge; and, when we came in sight of the people assembled there to witness the executions, they almost rent the air with shouts and exultations. I and my sixteen fellow-prisoners knelt down in a row. The blood of those who had been already executed on this spot (eighty-one in number) had more than stained, it streamed upon the ground about us. They first began the bloody tragedy by taking out Mr Daniels, who, the moment he was touched with their pikes, sprung over the battlements of the bridge into the waters, where he was instantly shot. Mr Robinson was the next: he was piked to death. The manner of piking was, by two of the rebels pushing their pikes into the front of the victim, while two others pushed pikes into his back, and in this state (writhing with torture) he was suspended aloft on the pikes till dead. He was then thrown over the bridge into the water. They ripped open the belly of poor Mr Atkins; and, in that condition, he ran several yards; when, falling on the side of the bridge, he was piked. Thus they proceeded till they came to Gurly, who was next to me. At that moment, one of them came up to me, and asked if I would have a priest. I felt my death to be certain, and I answered 'No'. He then pulled me by the collar; but it was desired to wait till Gurly was finished. While they were torturing him, General Roach rode up in great haste, and bid them beat to arms; informing them that Vinegar Hill camp was beset, and that reinforcements were wanting. This operated like lightening upon them: they all instantly quitted the bridge, and left Mr O'Connor, an organist; William Hamilton, the bailiff of the town; and myself, on our knees. The mob (consisting of more women than men) which had been spectators of this dreadful scene, also instantly dispersed in every direction, supposing the king's troops were at hand. We were so stupefied by terror that we remained for some time in this posture without making the least effort to escape. The rebel-guard soon came to us, and took us back to the gaol; telling us, that we should not escape longer than the next day, when neither man, woman, or child of the Protestants should be left alive. But it pleased God to prevent their dreadful intention from being carried into effect, by giving success to his Majesty's arms.

The main campaign in Wexford ended shortly after the narrow escape of Charles Jackson and his companions. Incidents of this nature were reciprocated by the victorious Loyalists as they reoccupied areas that had fallen to the rebels. The stories of atrocities helped to fuel inflamed sentiments against the native Irish, and it is significant that Jackson's account was published in Dublin before the end of the year. Reprisals accompanied the campaign of suppression, which continued for a considerable period of time afterwards, especially in the stronghold of the Wicklow mountains. The authorities could justifiably congratulate themselves, and their military commanders, on the successful conclusion of the struggle against the rebellion. The south-east was pacified, and also in the north-east of the country, the rising had been contained by July.

THE REBELLION IN THE NORTH-EAST

The United Irishmen rising in Ulster was timed to coincide approximately with other risings elsewhere in Ireland. Although Belfast was the cradle of the movement, for various reasons, the rebellion in Wexford, and later in the west of Ireland, has tended, unjustly, to overshadow until recently similar events in the north-east. The Nationalist tradition existed on resistant, if not hostile ground in the area in question. The great bulk of the songs and stories that recalled in later years the atmosphere and characters of "98', in the main refer to personalities of the south of Ireland. Yet in its time, the Ulster rebellion caused considerable worry to the Dublin authorities, until it became evident that the troops and their local supporters had succeeded in containing the United Irishmen in the area. In his correspondence with Sir Thomas Pelham, Viscount Castlereagh, in a letter dated 6 June 1798, refers in some detail to the military reverses that Loyalist forces were still continuing to suffer in Wexford:

> The rebellion seems to have taken serious root in Wexford. Their force is very great, the body in question exceeding ten thousand men, a considerable proportion of fire-arms, and conducted with attention to military principles.

The letter subsequently refers to the uneasy situation in the north, where the spirit of rebellion had begun to reveal itself:

> No disturbance has yet appeared in the other provinces, but my information from the north, this day received, makes it extremely to be apprehended that an effort will

shortly be made in that quarter. They only wait for a small co-operation from France, or some successes on the part of the southern rebels.

Dublin Castle was especially sensitive to the possibility of French military intervention in the growing internal conflict. England itself in that year was increasingly apprehensive of a French invasion. London was aware that Napoleon had assembled an army and a supporting naval force, but as yet it was impossible to determine where the enemy would choose to strike. Ireland in turmoil was one likely place to attempt a landing, in the hope of severing the island from England. Earl Camden, Lord-Lieutenant of Ireland, writing from Dublin Castle on 6 June to Pelham, voices official concern about the situation, with an urgent request that fresh troops be sent quickly from England to put down the rising in Ireland:

> The reason I so much press for this relief is the expectation that a landing, even of a small body of French, will set the country in a blaze, and I think neither our force nor our staff equal to the very difficult circumstances they will have to encounter.

Also writing to Thomas Pelham on 3 June William Elliot, under-secretary of the military department, expressed similar preoccupations, with a professional awareness of the amount of actual French help that might be required to affect the fortunes of the rebellion:

> The contest is yet by no means decided, but, if the rebels should not have the co-operation of a French army, I trust we shall put them down. If the French should be able to throw a force of five thousand men on any part of our coasts, it would render the result very dubious.

It was against this confused background that the northern United Irishmen rebellion got under way. The battle of Antrim was an outstanding engagement which, if it had succeeded in a manner similar to a number of the clashes in the Wexford area, would have affected considerably the outcome of the rising in general. There was at the time no sign of the expected French aid, and the northern rebels were isolated from those of the south and unable to join forces. A first-hand account of the battle comes from one of the major participants in the northern rebellion, James Hope. He claims that the persecution the people endured from the military was, as also in the south-east, a major cause of provoking the rebellion among the Ulster people:

We were thus situated, forced by burning of houses, and the torturing of the peasantry, into resistance. Without the due appointment of superior officers in the place of those who had resigned and abandoned the cause. I have already given you some account of the battle of Antrim; on some points, and not unimportant ones, you were misinformed by the Rev. Mr M'Cartney. I was present on that occasion, and not a mere spectator of that battle. I pointed out to you, on the spot, the ground we occupied, and the several places where our people, at the onset, had triumphantly charged their enemies, and had been at last repulsed by them. Previous to our march for Antrim I was not appointed to any command; I had refused to accept of any. In the front rank there were eighteen men, most of them personal friends and acquaintances of my own, led by a man named John M'Gladdery. I was in that front rank; and it was allowed by our opponents the men belonging to it marched up the main street, and met the enemies troops in good order, and did the duty assigned to them in a becoming manner. The first position taken was the church-yard, which commands the main street. There our green banner was unfurled, and M'Cracken was stationed with his principal officers about him.

When the street firing on us commenced, a girl came up to us, in the church-yard, and told our leader there was a loop-hole in the wall where he had better go. She had come there in the midst of the firing to point it out to him. When the panic occurred, and the party in reserve mistook the flight of some dragoons for a charge on their companions, M'Cracken on quitting the church-yard to check the disorder, left me in command of that place, and I maintained it as long as there was a hope of keeping possession of the town.

I wish to correct a few errors in the statement of Dr Macartney's, respecting the battle of Antrim. It is not true, that we had two pieces of cannon at Antrim, we had a brass piece which had belonged to the Volunteers. It, and another of the same description, had been buried without the knowledge of the Rev. Mr Campbell, in his Meeting House at Templepatrick. When the Monaghan Militia were burning the village of Templepatrick, the other piece was discovered, and Mr Campbell, who knew nothing whatsoever of the concealment of the two pieces there, was suspected to have had a guilty knowledge of the fact, and was never forgiven by Lord Templeton. The men who were in the foremost ranks of the people, marching into Antrim, were a small body of the Roughforth Volunteers, remarkably steady men, they came on in three files, six deep. The column that followed consisted of Templepatrick and Carmoney men, and some of the Killead people, who had arms. Those of the Campbell family were particularly distinguished among them for their courage; Joshua and Henry fell in the action.

It is stated by Mr Macartney, that the people marched to music, or that the air of the Lass of Richmond Hill was played. We had no musical instruments of any kind amongst us. A man of the name of Harvey commenced singing 'The Marsellois Hymn', as we marched into the town, in which his companions joined, but thinking we needed a more lively air, I struck up a verse of a merry

Irish song, which was soon joined in by our party.

Mr Macartney, and the yeomen he commanded, after the burning of some houses in the town, had taken refuge behind the wall of the park of Lord Massarene, in front of the high street, and occasionally rose up and fired some shots down the street. Close to the market-house, near the castle gate, some yeomen and horse soldiers kept their ground, the yeomen had two pieces of cannon there, which were soon silenced. We were about to attack the horsemen when a body of Ballyclare men entered the town by the west end street, and by Bow-lane. This caused some confusion, and the troops at the market-house profited by it to renew their fire, and took off some of our leaders. The people began to give way, and in attempting to stop the fugitives, M'Cracken, who proceeding with a party of men, by the rear of the houses, to dislodge the yeomen stationed in Lord Massarene's park, was borne down, disobeyed, and deserted by the panic struck multitude. He then made his way to Donogore Hill, along with Robert Wilson, where he expected to find a body of men in reserve, but all his plans had been frustrated by the defection of the military chiefs. James Agnew Farrel, and Mr Quin, a person employed in the salt works at Larne, had been appointed colonels, but neither acted. Farrel either brought, or sent, his fighting orders to General Nugent, and then he went to Scotland. One of our prisoners was a Captain George Mason M'Claverty, who had been taken that morning in his house, and carried to Donegal Hill. He used every argument to prevail on the people to disperse and return to their homes, promising them every protection in his power. He subsequently fulfilled his promise to the letter, not one of the persons in his neighbourhood, many of whom he had seen in arms that day, did he suffer to be troubled or persecuted. He was one to the most humane and just magistrates in the county. The number of people killed in the town, that is to say in the action, was very few. James M'Glathery, who had a command, wrote a sketch of the action, which Miss M'Cracken saw in the

71

hands of his sister, Mrs Shaw, of Belfast, in which it was stated that only five or six of the people were killed in the town in action, and H. J. M'Cracken said the statement was correct. The dead bodies of both parties were buried in the sands, at Shane's Castle, but those of the people, who were found slain in the fields, were buried in the cross roads at Muckamore, where it had been customary to inter those who committed suicide.

While any prospect of serving our cause appeared to exist, a few of us remained in arms; our ranks at length diminished, the influence of the merchants on the manufacturers, and that of the manufacturers on the workmen, formed a strong claim of pecuniary interests in the province of Ulster, so that shelter or relief of any kind afforded to those who stood out, was at the risk of the life and property of the giver.

The very perfection of our organization in Ulster gave treachery the greater scope, from the greater intercourse it caused in societies and committees, and numbers of persons, thus becoming personally known to each other, the organization of treachery was rendered still more complete, and, if a comparative few had not thrown their lives into the scale, Castlereagh's plan of keeping the north and south divided, must have sooner succeeded.

When all our leaders deserted us, Henry Joy M'Cracken stood alone faithful to the last. He led on the forlorn hope of the cause at Antrim, and brought the government to terms with all but the leaders.

He died, rather than prove a traitor to his cause, of which fact I am still a living witness, who shared in all his exertions while he lived, and defy any authentic contradiction of that assertion now, or at any future date.

James Hope's further narrative of the encounter at Ballymena on 7 June is perhaps more dramatic than his somewhat reflective account of the important battle of Antrim. The latter report however contains a number of conclusions that help the reader to understand the northern situation more completely: the official policy of ensuring that the two parts of the island remained as far as possible cut off from each other, to minimise the effect of the Rising; the problems of inadequate training and poor armament which also dogged the rebels' efforts in the south; the fact that their French allies did not put in an appearance in time to be of use to the rebellions of early summer; and, especially in the north, the desertion of the United Irishmen movement by large numbers of its former adherents, discouraged by official harassment and in many cases absorbed into the anti-Republican ranks of the Orange Societies. These were particularly powerful in the north, but a considerable body of southern Protestants also belonged to the anti-revolutionary organisation, giving a certain quality of a religious war to the rebellion. This aspect of the situation was stressed by William Elliot in the letter quoted previously, referring to the Wexford campaign:

> The war in that part of the country has certainly assumed a strong religious spirit, and I cannot help suspecting that the Orange associations, which, you will recollect, were formed and promoted by Colonel Rochfort and some other gentlemen in the counties of Wexford and Carlow, operated very mischievously. This, however, you will observe, is merely my own suspicion, and I can really give you no particular facts to support my opinion. Lord Fingal and most of the leading persons of the Catholic persuasion have presented a very loyal and spirited address, and, I believe, are perfectly impressed with the danger which is menaced to all religion and to all property. Among the lower class of the Catholics there appears to be a very widely extended disaffection, and it will be indubitably the object of the chiefs of the rebellion to fan the flame of religious dissension, which the foolish and acrimonious conversation and conduct of the intemperate part of the Protestants will not tend to abate.

Religious conflict, underlying the element of class conflict of which the under-secretary was aware, complicated and intensified the rebellion in the south. In the north, it possibly contributed to the relatively rapid suppression of the rising. Little more than a week after his expressions of grave misgivings with regard to affairs in the north, Viscount Castlereagh could write to the same William Elliot, to inform the latter that the military campaign against the Ulster rebels was already having better results than in Wexford:

> The operations in the north have so far been very favourable; we have succeeded in giving the rebels, both in Down and Antrim, a severe check, which, considering the reduced state of Nugent's force, and the serious consequences that might have resulted from any reverse in that quarter (where troops were not immediately at hand to repair a disaster), is in itself an important advantage, though it by no means ensures the suppression of the rebellion, nor can it be looked to as securing us against its extension to the other counties of the provinces.
>
> The rebels fought at Ballynahinch (Co. Down), as in Wexford, with determined bravery, but without the fanaticism of the southerns. They made the attack and used some of the wretched ship guns mounted on cars with considerable address. The body there assembled was entirely dispersed; in their ranks were found two of my father's servants, a footman and postilion. The rebels are in possession of the Ards, and their force considerable on the mountain above Newtownards.
>
> Upon the whole the north is divided in sentiment. We have numerous adherents, and I am inclined to hope that the effort there will prove rather a diversion than the main attack ....

In view of the situation in Wexford when the above letter was being written (15 June) Castlereagh had reason to feel more confident of being able to bring matters to a rapid conclusion in the government's favour in Ulster. Apart from personal recollections of the fighting and the tone of official correspondence, one particularly poignant eyewitness document emerged from 1798 in the north. Perhaps the most outstanding name associated with the rebellion is that of James Hope's friend and companion-in-arms, Henry Joy M'Cracken. As Hope expressed it: 'faithful to the last', for which M'Cracken paid the supreme penalty, as did also many others whose names turn up in General Lake's reports to Dublin Castle. His devoted sister, Mary, left an account of her last meeting with her brother, shortly before he went to the gallows:

During the early part of the day Harry and I had conversed with tranquillity on the subject of his death. We had been brought up in a firm conviction of an all-wise and overruling Providence, and of the duty of entire resignation to the Divine will. I remarked that his death was as much a dispensation of Providence as if it happened in the common course of nature, to which he assented. He told me that there had been much perjury on his trial, but that the truth would have answered the same purpose. After the clergymen were gone, I asked for a pair of scissors, that I might take off some of his hair. A young officer who was on guard (his name was George) went out of the room and brought a pair of scissors, but hesitated to trust them into my hand, when I asked him indignantly if he thought I meant to hurt my brother. He then gave them to me, and I cut off some of Harry's hair which curled round his neck, and folded it up in paper, and put it into my bosom. Fox at that moment entered the room, and desired me to give it to him, as 'too much use,' he said, 'had already been made of such things'. I refused, saying I would only part with it in death; when my dear brother said, 'Oh, Mary, give it to him; of what value is it?' I felt that its possession would be a mere gratification to me, and, not wishing to discompose him by the contest, I gave it up.

The time allowed him was now expired: he had hoped for a few days, that he might give his friends an account of all the late events in which he had taken a part. About 5p.m. he was ordered to the place of execution, the old market-house, the ground of which had been given to the town by his great great grandfather. I took his arm, and we walked together to the place of execution, where I was told it was the General's orders I should leave him, which I peremptorily refused. Harry begged I would go. Clasping my hands around him (I did not weep till then), I said I could bear any thing but leaving him. Three times he kissed me, and entreated I would go; and, looking round to recognise some friend to put me in charge of, he beckoned to a Mr Boyd, and said, 'He will take charge of you'. Mr Boyd stepped forward and, fearing any further refusal would disturb the last moments of my dearest brother, I suffered myself to be led away. Mr Boyd endeavoured to give me comfort, and I felt there was still comfort in the hope he gave me, that we should meet in heaven. A Mr Armstrong, a friend of our family, came forward and took me from Mr Boyd, and conducted me home. I immediately sent a message to Dr M'Donnell and Mr M'Cluney, our apothecary, to come directly to the house. The latter came, and Dr M'Donnell sent his brother Alexander, a skilful surgeon. The body was given up to his family unmutilated; so far our entreaties and those of our friends prevailed.

THE REBELLION IN THE
WEST: INVASION

Mary M'Cracken had evidently thought of attempting to resuscitate her brother, in the hope that he might not be completely dead having been hanged. There had been attested cases of the successful reanimating of persons officially pronounced dead by hanging. Her desperate hopes proved to be in vain, and her brother became one of the martyrs of Irish nationalism for later generations. By late July of that year, many of the principal leaders of the insurrection were also dead, the people apparently cowed and glad to remain docile and escape reprisals. Most of the surviving rank and file of the rising had returned home wherever possible, to attend to their neglected fields and the harvests. The authorities could relax, at least for the moment, in the knowledge that the king's troops had put down the rebellion in the areas where it had been most serious and threatening. The army was also engaged in reducing the remaining pockets of United Irishmen resistance in the Wicklow mountains. At the same time, the reprisals continued unabated, keeping the native population under control. Then suddenly, in the month of August, the frightening news reached Dublin that the long-expected French invasion force had finally landed, in the far west of Ireland, and that Napoleon's troops, together with a further rebel horde from that previously undisturbed part of the country, were marching on Dublin itself. The principal and most reliable eyewitness of the French invasion and many of the events in the west of Ireland, was the Protestant bishop of Killala, Joseph Stock. His personal account of the episode was published anonymously in 1800, and this was followed by later editions. His narrative is a lively, fair-minded and penetrating recollection of the agitated weeks of the invasion and the eventual defeat of the rising in Connaught. The bishop noted with considerable detail the various aspects of the initial French presence in Mayo, as their general took the first steps towards securing the country for his campaign. The French were well organised, bringing arms, clothing and money for potential recruits, and further material was expected from France at any moment. Appropriately, the green flag was hoisted bearing the motto ERIN GO BRAGH (for which the bishop required a translation), while the spirit of the French Revolution of 1789 became the rallying-cry of the native Irish who flocked to join their allies:

> In war, it is said, the first success is every thing. The maxim was at least verified here by the instant accession of many hundreds of the country people to the cause of the French, which they affected to style the cause of Ireland.
>
> Chests each containing forty fusils, and others filled with new French uniforms and gaudy helmets, being heaped together in the castle-yard, the first that offered their service received complete clothing; and these, by credible report, were about a thousand in number. The next comers, who were at least as many, had every thing but shoes and stockings. To the last, arms only were given. And of arms Col Charost assured the bishop not less than 5,500 stand were in this place delivered out to the insurgents. The musquets were pronounced, by those who were judges of them, to be well fabricated, though their bore was too small to admit English bullets. The carabines were remarkable for their goodness. Swords and pistols, of which there was no great plenty, were reserved as marks of distinction, to be distributed only to the rebel officers.
>
> It was a melancholy spectacle to those in the castle, to witness the eagerness with which the unfortunate rustics

pressed forward to lay hold of these fatal trappings, the sure harbingers of their own speedy destruction. A very little penetration was required to discover the madness of expecting final success in such an enterprise, conducted by such a force, against an army at that time in the kingdom of probably not less than a hundred thousand men. But though the bait was visible to people of any sense, to the multitude it certainly was in no small degree alluring.

The uncombed ragged peasant, who had never before known the luxury of shoes and stockings, now washed, powdered, and full dressed, was metamorphosed into another being, the rather because the far greater part of these mountaineers were by no means deficient either in size or in person. 'Look at those poor fellows,' said Humbert with an air of triumph to the bishop, 'they are made, you find, of the same stuff with ourselves.' A still stronger temptation offered itself to people unaccustomed to animal food, in a full enjoyment of fresh meat. The lowest allowance of beef for a day was one pound to each recruit. This was devoured with an avidity, that excited sometimes the mirth, sometimes the contempt of their French associates. A French officer protested, that having for curiosity trusted an Irishman at once with an allowance of eight pounds of dressed meat, he saw the creature throw himself on the ground, and begin to gnaw it so eagerly, that he was sure he would not rise till he had consumed it.

Taking such minor incidents into account, one is sometimes led to the conclusion that their English opponents on occasion felt a certain admiration, however grudgingly, for their United Irishmen enemies, which the latters' French allies did not often share. Certainly there were considerable cultural gaps between the native Irish and the French invaders, which took the latter by surprise. Contributing to these almost insurmountable cultural distinctions, was the deep-rooted religious presence among the Irish, a factor which Bishop Stock noted from the outset:

Indeed, the contrast with regard to religious sentiments, between the French and their Irish allies, was extremely curious. The atheist despised and affronted the bigot; but the wonder was how the zealous papist should come to any terms of agreement with a set of men, who boasted openly in our hearing, 'that they had just driven Mr POPE out of Italy, and did not expect to find him again so suddenly in Ireland'. It astonished the French officers to hear the recruits, when they offered their service, declare, 'that they were come to take arms for France and the blessed Virgin'.

The French, true to the anti-clerical principles of the Revolution, did not hesitate to show their open contempt for those members of the Irish clergy who joined the ranks of the United Irishmen forces. These rebels of the west of Ireland, Bishop Stock, insisted, showed none of the savagery towards Protestants and Loyalists that had tarnished the idealism of the rebellion in Wexford. He attributes this restraint in part to the presence of French officers who exercised greater control over their Irish recruits. The French were contending with specific problems, such as the lack of military training and experience that made it difficult at times to deploy the growing number of rebels effectively. Added to this factor was the question of insufficient discipline and a certain element of unpredictable behaviour in men who found the atmosphere of warfare heady, especially when they got their unaccustomed hands on firearms. The United Irishmen leader, Thomas Cloney, recalled how he experienced a similar difficulty with the men under his command:

> I have often been surprised that accidents among our rude, and often ungovernable, troops were not more frequent, as it was the ambition of every stripling to have a musket or pistol, to carry a pike being considered a mark

of their inferiority as soldiers. Many of those who became possessors of firearms by their courage, were ignorant of their use, and never did children show more eagerness in examining their newly purchased toys, than did such men in firing with their recently acquired instruments of death. In the camp and on the march they could not easily be restrained from using them in this way, and having too often and too freely indulged in the use of spirituous liquors, this practice of voluntary firing became very dangerous.

Whatever the problems of attempting to organise an effective army out of such a force, the French and Irish combined army initially obtained notable successes against the English, who were relatively unprepared for serious action in the west and who were also taken by surprise by the course of events. Successes such as the famous 'Races of Castlebar' have been documented, as also other encounters during the march on Dublin. Although the rising in that part of Ireland consisted, above all, of a military campaign, it was equally a matter of nationalism. At Castlebar the Republic of Connaught was proclaimed, with John Moore, of Moore Hall on the shores of Lough Carra, Co. Mayo, as its President – in theory, the first president of Ireland. It was intended that the provisional Republic of Connaught would expand to become the Republic of Ireland after the victorious conclusion of the rebellion. The unfortunate John Moore paid the price of many other United Irishmen leaders taken prisoner in the rising.

In addition to the problem of organising an untrained horde against experienced soldiers, there was also the fact that the French force that had landed numbered about one thousand men, a figure considerably below the five thousand which William Elliot estimated to be the most effective invasion force. By the time they had crossed the Shannon and reached the neighbourhood of Longford, their Irish allies were beginning to desert the French and the remainder were beginning to feel campaign exhaustion. They were now faced by fresh, well armed enemy troops brought up from the recently pacified south-east and elsewhere. England had already sent Lord Cornwallis to Ireland as commander-in-chief, and the able Generals Lake and Moore marched their regiments from the south. A very superior English force met the French and their Irish allies near Granard, a little to the north-east of Longford town. There a brief battle took place, and the French surrendered. As gallant enemy soldiers they were granted the usual terms of capitulation, but it is recorded that no terms were offered to the Irish rebels, who were forced to make a stand and who were indiscriminately massacred on the spot. This evidently was intended to be part of the lesson in subordination that was applied to the insurgents. A telling detail from General Sir John Moore's account from his diaries of the defeat of the invaders, refers to the ground covered the next day by the bodies of slaughtered rebels, but makes no mention of French corpses:

Whilst this was being carried out (i.e., the march to Boyle) we were informed of the particulars of an action that had happened the day before between the French and three hundred of the Limerick City Militia, who had marched from Sligo under Colonel Verecker to attack them. The Militia were not only outnumbered, but had not taken advantage of the ground. They had been beaten, and had lost their two guns, and sixty men had been made prisoners. Wrong information of the number of the enemy had induced the Colonel to volunteer this attack. I encamped about five miles from Colloney, eight miles from Boyle. We here heard that numbers of the rebels were leaving the French, and had been seen crossing the country towards

Mayo. Some of the yeomen brought in as prisoners several of them whom they had found in arms. The inhabitants in the county of Sligo appeared to be more loyal than I had observed the people to be elsewhere. The Orange faction is, I understand, strong. On the 8th I marched to Carrick-on-Shannon. The French had passed the Shannon at Ballintra the day before. They had attempted to destroy the bridge, but had been prevented doing so by Colonel Crauford with the cavalry of General Lake's advanced guard. The French had marched on Mohill and Granard; Lake had followed them. Lord Cornwallis, after resting his army for some hours, had marched at 10p.m. to Mohill. The orders he left for me were that I was to issue such orders for the regulation of the garrison of Carrick, and for the care of ammunition and stores, as I thought expedient, and then, after refreshing my men, pursue such measures and route as should appear to me best calculated for the general good. In the course of the day I received intelligence of the surrender of the French after a partial action with General Lake's advanced guard at Ballinamuck, between Mohill and Granard. Colonel Crauford with the cavalry, and particularly with the detachment of the Hompesch he took from me, had hung upon the rear of the French for two days, and had so harassed them as to be the immediate cause of their surrender; but at any rate they could not have escaped Lord Cornwallis's column, which had already reached St Johnston at the time of the surrender.

On the 9th General Hewitt wrote to me from the camp at Johnston that Lord Cornwallis was going to Lord Longford's, near Castle Pollard, and desired to see me as soon as possible. Here my brother James left me and returned to London. I rode that night to Mohill. I was tired and not well from sleeping on wet ground the night before, and I required a good bed, which I got at Mohill. Next morning I rode through General Lake's camp over the ground where the action had taken place; it was covered with dead rebels. I reached Packenham Hall by breakfast time.

Lord Cornwallis had at first intended to have me sent to Castlebar and Killala to settle and disarm that part of the country; but he received from the Duke of Portland information, which he showed me, of an armament being ready in Brest to sail for this country. This determined him to send General Trench on that service and to keep my corps in a central situation near Kilbeggan or Moate. The destination of the different corps of the army was decided in the course of that day.

There is another account of the French landing at Killala and the subsequent campaign that ended near Granard. It comes from the memoirs of the ubiquitous Moreau de Jonnés, who also claimed to have played a role of some importance in the second French expedition to Ireland. Again, this is a mixture of fact and obvious fiction, with predominance being given to the latter element. His narrative leans heavily on the combination of adventure and romance that characterises his earlier account of the expedition to Bantry Bay, and apart from presenting a possible basis for a novel or a film script, Moreau de Jonnés' personal story adds little or nothing to the picture provided by more reliable eyewitnesses. His most interesting comment is a passing disparaging reference to the French commander, General Humbert, whom he considered to be inadequate to the situation : 'It is probable that General Humbert, instead of being well read in Frederick 2nd. and Montécuculi, had never opened a book since he left school'.

The novelist, Maria Edgeworth, provides a more realistic account of the final hours of the 1798 rebellion, as witnessed by her in Longford town, where she and her family had taken refuge having fled from Edgeworthstown before the advancing rebel forces. In Longford she witnessed the arrival of some of the French prisoners taken at Ballinamuck, but at the time a crisis connected with the rebellion had arisen for members of her family, which required the whole of her attention. A Loyalist lynch-mob accused her father of being an agent for the French and a traitor to the king. He needed the protection of English army officers in order to appear personally in the street, while all around the victory jubilations were taking place. The homicidal fury of the mob, incensed by their recent feelings of terror, nearly proved fatal to the novelist's father:

We heard my father in the evening ask Major Eustace, to walk with him through the town to the barrack-yard to evening parade; and we saw them go out together without feeling the slightest apprehension. We remained at the inn. By this time Col Handfield, Major Cannon, and some other officers, had arrived, and they were at the inn at dinner in a parlour on the ground floor, under our room. It being hot weather, the windows were open. Nothing now seemed to be thought of but rejoicings for the victory. Candles were preparing for the illumination; waiters, chambermaids, landlady, all hands were busy scooping turnips and potatoes for candlesticks, to stand in every pane of every loyal window.

In the midst of this preparation about half an hour after my father had left us, we heard a great uproar in the street. At first we thought that the shouts were only rejoicings for victory, but as they came nearer we heard screechings and yellings, indescribably horrible. A mob had gathered at the gates of the barrack-yard, and joined by many soldiers of the yeomanry on leaving parade, had followed Major Eustace and my father from the barracks. The major being this evening in coloured clothes, the people no longer knew him to be an officer nor conceived, as they had done before, that Mr Edgeworth was his prisoner. The mob had not contented themselves with the horrid yells that we had heard, but had been pelting them with hard turf, stones, and brickbats. From one of these my father received a blow on the side of his head, which came with such force as to stagger, and almost to stun him; but he kept himself from falling, knowing that if once he fell he should be trampled under foot. He walked on steadily until he came within a few yards of the inn, when one of the mob seized hold of Major Eustace by the collar. My father seeing the windows of the inn open, called with a loud voice, 'Major Eustace is in danger!' The officers, who were at dinner, and who till that moment had supposed the noise in the street to be only drunken rejoicings, immediately ran out, and rescued Major Eustace and my father. At the sight of British officers and drawn swords, the populace gave way, and dispersed in different directions.

The preparations for the illuminations then went on, as if nothing had intervened. All the panes of the windows in the front room were in a blaze of light the time the mob returned through the street. The night passed without further disturbance.

As early as we could the next morning we left Longford, and returned homewards, all danger from the rebels being now over, and the rebellion having been terminated by the late battle.

THE AFTERMATH OF THE REBELLION

Maria Edgeworth was correct in assuming that the rebellion had in effect finished. The defeat of the rebel forces was decisive and the survivors were being hunted throughout the west, as they had previously been in the north and the south-east. The remainder of the native population was cowed by the turn of events and, above all, the fact that now the most extreme Loyalist elements in the country could act with impunity against them. Apart from a few brief visits by French ships to the Irish shores, the threat from France had receded. Napoleon had turned his main attention to Egypt, where the military situation was not turning out in his favour – news had reached Ireland of admiral Nelson's naval victory over the French at the mouth of the Nile, at about the same time as the French capitulation at Ballinamuck. What remained was the task of pacification, a mopping-up process accompanied by the sort of individual violence and vindictiveness that Maria Edgeworth had briefly glimpsed at Longford.

Bishop Stock of Killala was witness to the reprisals and executions that followed on the rebel defeat, in spite of the fact, as the bishop took pains to point out, the insurgents in the west of Ireland in general behaved relatively well towards the Loyalist population of the area during their short period of triumph. The bishop in his account of the episode admonishes the foolhardy who were so ready to rush into civil war, but he nevertheless expresses sympathy for those now forced to pay the price of their political recklessness:

What heart can forget the impression it has received from

the glance of a fellow creature, pleading for his life, with a crowd of bayonets at his breast? The eye of Demosthenes never emitted so penetrating a beam, in his most enraptured flight of oratory. Such a man was dragged before the bishop on the day after the battle (i.e., at Killala), while the hand of slaughter was still in pursuit of unresisting peasants through the town. In the agonies of terror the prisoner thought to save his life by crying out, 'that he was known to the bishop.' Alas! the bishop knew him not; neither did he look like a good man. But the arms and the whole body of the person to whom he flew for protection were over him immediately. Memory suggested rapidly: 'what a piece of workship is man! the beauty of the world, the paragon of animals! ...

'And are you going to deface this admirable work!' As indeed they did. For though the soldiers promised to let the unfortunate man remain in custody till he should have a trial, yet when they found he was not known, they pulled him out of the court-yard, as soon as the bishop's back was turned, and shot him at the gate.

Bishop Stock did not witness the worst of the atrocities, but as the summer passed, these eventually diminished, but not before even the extreme Loyalist and adherent of the Orange societies, Sir Jonah Barrington, was forced to admit that his co-religionaries were overdoing their policy of suppression: 'I must in truth and candour say, (and I say it with reluctance) that, during those most sanguinary scenes, the brutal conduct of certain frantic Royalists was at least on a parallel with that of the frantic rebels'. By the autumn of 1798 it would seem that the country had finally seen 'an end of Popery's persecuting reign', to quote the words of one contemporary Loyalist historian of the rising, George Taylor. There remained for long after the event a residue on all sides of the conflicting sentiments that had made the fight intensely bitter for many participants and eyewitnesses. Over two decades later, Crofton Croker was able to record that the political and religious differences that the rising had forced to the surface, 'are not forgotten to the present hour'.

There were also physical consequences of the rebellion to take note of. The Rev. James Hall, touring Ireland in 1807, recorded that '... hares, rabbits, partridges, grouse, and other animals, alarmed at the tremendous burnings, fled the county, and have not yet returned.' In her recollections, Mary Leadbeater mentions a still more unpleasant physical consequence of the battles: 'For several months there was no sale for bacon cured in Ireland, from the well founded dread of the hogs having fed upon the flesh of men'.

Apart from the undercurrent of attitudes that the rising had bequeathed to the following generation and even to those who came much later, the most important immediate consequence of 1798, was the Act of Union of 1801. The English authorities took full advantage of the situation to push through legislation against considerable internal Irish opposition, that abolished the Parliament in Dublin and made Ireland an integral part of the United Kingdom. From that moment on, political power lay exclusively with Westminster and any future attempt to achieve independence by rebellion in Ireland would meet head-on the full might of the British Empire. For England the events of 1798 had revealed the inability of a native Irish government to contain sedition and rebellion. The links between the Irish rebels and England's enemies abroad also posed a major potential threat for national security. In spite of the turn of events in the political and administrative field, there was nevertheless a further attempt at rebellion in Ireland, on the heels, as it were, of the defeat of 1798.

In 1803 in Dublin, Robert Emmet and his fellow-conspirators, among them Myles Byrne and other surviving United

Irishmen, initiated a short-lived rising. Its collapse, followed by Emmet's trial and execution, brought an end to the spirit of '98 – at least, for a time. The passage of the years revealed that the nationalism born of 1798 was exceptionally tenacious and it survived, mainly among certain minority groups, into the twentieth century. Whereas for many people in the nineteenth century the question of the rebellion for long remained a matter to instil a sense of shame, for others the rising became the main source of inspiration of their actions. It came to represent the nation that might have been, had the worst fears of Dublin Castle become fact. Daniel O'Connell and his supporters rejected the violent solution to Ireland's problems and sought to have the Act of Union repealed by constitutional means. The Young Irelanders of the 1840s, and the Fenians of a generation later, believed in the need for an armed rebellion in order to throw off English rule. For these radical nationalist groups, the insurrection of 1798 was their ideal and the model to emulate. It provided later generations of Irish rebels with the outstanding martyrs and heroes of the Nationalist cause: Wolfe Tone, Lord Edward Fitzgerald, Henry Joy M'Cracken, Robert Emmet and others. The names of those considered to have sacrificed their lives for Ireland's freedom became the subjects of song and story, even legend, and were sometimes surrounded by an aura of romance.

The political and social situation within Ireland did not necessarily improve, in spite of the change of the seat of authority. One might perhaps claim with some justification that matters in certain areas became worse than before. Although the process of subduing the native Irish population after the rising had been exceptionally severe and intense, within a generation agrarian disturbances became as violent as in the previous century. Ireland remained a country prone to upheavals, of a local and a national nature, and a considerable body of armed police was required to keep the peace.

Throughout the nineteenth century, the Nationalist spirit that first manifested itself in 1798 kept flaring up. It survived the reversals suffered by radical groups, the Great Famine of the 1840s, the fall of Parnell and other vicissitudes. The continual failure to achieve progress by constitutional means also helped to keep the spirit of rebellion alive for many. Its contribution to the evolution of modern Irish nationalism has been amply recognised by many commentators. As the historian, G. A. Hayes-McCoy has put it, writing well within the twentieth century: 'To us, the rebellion of 1798, as well as being the last Irish war until our own day, is the first with a recognisable aim.' The late nineteenth century witnessed a certain liberalisation of Irish affairs and more than once Westminster had broached the idea of Home Rule for Ireland, but without attaining concrete results other than rejection of the proposal. Nationalist aspirations in Ireland continued to feel the distant influence of 1798, which became especially palpable as the nation approached the first centenary of the rising. Joseph H. Fowler recalled in later years the heady ideological atmosphere of the occasion, as he experienced it during his youth: 'In the centenary year, a lad of 15, my imagination was fired by the stirring events, recalled by the poetry and prose of patriotic writers and the great hostings that met on the battlefields of '98. Monuments to the leaders of the Insurrection were erected throughout the land, from Kildare to Arklow, and there was a tremendous revival of the nationalist ideal'. The revival evolved into the movements that produced the major national events of the twentieth century, from the creation of a strong Republican movement to the Easter Rising of 1916 and the ensuing War of Independence. Those are other matters, which lie outside the scope of this volume.

BIBLIOGRAPHICAL SOURCES

Adams, Jane: *Personal Narrative, etc.* See: Crofton-Croker, T.: *Researches in the South of Ireland*

Alexander, James: *Some Account of the first apparent symptoms of the late Rebellion in the county of Kildare (and) in the county of Wexford especially in the vicinity of Ross.* John Jones, Dublin 1800.

Barrington, Sir Jonah: *Personal Sketches and Recollections of his own Times.* Cameron, Ferguson & Co., Glasgow 1827

Byrne, Miles: *Some Notes of an Irish Exile of 1798.* Maunsel & Co. Ltd. Dublin (n.d.)

Castlereagh, Viscount, 2nd Marquess of Londonderry: *Memoirs and Correspondence of...*, edited by his brother, Charles Vane, Marquess of Londonderry. Henry Colburn, London 1848.

Cloney, Thomas: *A Personal Narrative of those Transactions in the County Wexford during 1798.* Dublin 1832.

Crofton-Croker, T.: *Researches in the South of Ireland.* John Murray, London 1824. Jane Adam's narrative is published as an appendix to the main text.

Cullen, Brother Luke, ODC: "98 in Wicklow'. *The People* Newspapers Ltd. Wexford 1938.

De Latocnaye: *A Frenchman's Walk through Ireland 1796–97.* Trans. by John Stevenson. Hodges Figgis & Co. Ltd. Dublin 1917. Also: Blackstone Press, 1984, with an introduction by John A. Gamble, FRGS.

Edgeworth, Maria: *Life and Letters of ...* Edward Arnold, London 1824.

Farrell, William: *Carlow in '98.* Edited by Roger J. McHugh. Browne & Nolan Ltd. The Richview Press, Dublin 1949.

Fowler, Joseph H.: *Chapters in '98 History, 1798–1938.* St Giles Bookshop, London.

Gilbert, John J. (ed.): *Documents relating to Ireland 1795–1804.*

Irish University Press, Shannon 1970. First edition Dublin 1893.

Hall, Rev. J.: *A Tour through Ireland in 1807*. London 1813.

Hayes-McCoy, G. A.: *Irish Battles*. Longmans, Green & Co. Ltd. London 1969.

Holt, Joseph: *Memoirs of Joseph Holt General of the Irish Rebels in 1798*. Ed. T. Crofton-Croker, Esq. Henry Colburn Publisher, London 1838.

Hope, James: See: Dr. Madden: *Antrim and Down in '98*.

Jackson, Charles: *Narrative of the Sufferings and Escape of Charles Jackson*. J. Milliken, Grafton Street Dublin 1798.

Leadbeater, Mary: *Annals of Ballitore*. Bell & Daldy, London 1862.

Lecky, W. H. E.: *A History of Ireland in the Eighteenth Century*. 5 vols. 1892–96. Longmans Green & Co. London 1906.

McCracken, Mary : See: Madden, Dr

Madden, Dr: *Antrim and Down in '98*. Burnes Oates & Washbourne Ltd. London n.d. The volume also contains James Hope's *Memoirs*.

Moore, General Sir John: *The Diary of Sir John Moore*. Edited by Major-General Sir J. F. Maurice, KCB. Edward Arnold, London 1904.

Moreau de Jonnés, A.: *Adventures in Wars of the Republic and Consulate*. John Murray, London 1920.

Stock, Joseph, Bishop of Killala: *A narrative of what passed at Killalla in the County of Mayo and Parts adjacent during the French Invasion in the Summer of 1798, by an Eyewitness*. Published anonymously by R. E. Mercier & Co. Dublin 1800. Various later editions in Ireland and in the UK. Republished 1982 by Irish Humanities Centre, Terrybaun, Bofeenaun, Ballina, Co. Mayo.

Taylor, George: *A History of the Rebellion in the county of Wexford in the year 1798*. Wm. Curry & Co. Dublin 1829.

Wolfe Tone, Theobald: *Autobiography*. Extracts from his Journals published by his son. L. Whittaker, Treacher & Arnot, London MDCCCXXX.

MORE INTERESTING BOOKS

THE COURSE OF IRISH HISTORY
EDITED BY T. W. MOODY AND F. X. MARTIN

This book provides a rapid short survey, with geographical introduction, of the whole course of Ireland's history. Based on a series of television programmes, it is designed to be both popular and authoritative, concise but comprehensive, highly selective but balanced and fair-minded, critical but constructive and sympathetic. A distinctive feature is its wealth of illustrations.

The present edition is a revised and enlarged version of the original book. New material has been added, bringing the narrative to the IRA ceasefire of 31 August 1994.

THE GREAT IRISH FAMINE
EDITED BY CATHAL PÓIRTÉIR

This is the most wide-ranging series of essays ever published on the Great Irish Famine and will prove of lasting interest to the general reader. Leading historians, economists, geographers – from Ireland, Britain and the United States – have assembled the most up-to-date research from a wide spectrum of disciplines, including medicine, folklore and literature, to give the fullest account yet of the background and consequences of the Famine.

THE PATH TO FREEDOM
MICHAEL COLLINS

Many books have been written about the life and death of Michael Collins. *The Path to Freedom* is the only book he wrote himself.

These articles and speeches, first published in 1922, throw light not only on the War of Independence, the Civil War and the foundation of the Free State but on crucial contemporary issues.

> The actions taken indicated an over-keen desire for peace, and although terms of truce were virtually agreed upon, they were abandoned because the British leaders thought their actions indicated weakness, and they consequently decided to insist upon the surrender of our arms. The result was the continuance of the struggle.

Michael Collins on efforts to bring about a truce earlier in 1920.

Michael Collins
The Man Who Won the War
T. Ryle Dwyer

In formally proposing the adoption of the Anglo-Irish Treaty on 19 December 1921 Arthur Griffith referred to Michael Collins as 'the man who won the War', much to the annoyance of the Defence Minister Cathal Brugha, who questioned whether Collins 'had ever fired a shot at any enemy of Ireland'.

Who was this Michael Collins, and what was his real role in the War of Independence? How was it that two sincere, selfless individuals like Griffith and Brugha, could differ so strongly about him?

This is the story of a charismatic rebel who undermined British morale and inspired Irish people with exploits, both real and imaginary. He co-ordinated the sweeping Sinn Féin election victory of 1918, organised the IRA, set up the first modern intelligence network, masterminded a series of prison escapes and supervised the fundraising to finance the movement.

Collins probably never killed anybody himself, but he did order the deaths of people standing in his way, and even advocated kidnapping an American President. He was the prototype of the urban terrorist and the real architect of the Black and Tan War.